10-12-96

Dear Joyce and David,

You have always been a big part of our own education of the heart. From the first time I met you in Seattle, through the Rochester years, the Irvine visits, and now here together in Utah Valley.

I hope you enjoy the book. Love,

Russ

THE

EDUCATION

OF THE

HEART

*Rediscovering the Spiritual
Roots of Learning*

THE
EDUCATION
OF THE
HEART

Rediscovering the Spiritual
Roots of Learning

RUSSELL T. OSGUTHORPE

Covenant Communications, Inc.

To Lolly,
my companion in the search
who teaches me
daily
that two can learn as one,
cleaving to truth and to each other
forever

Published by Covenant Communications, Inc.
American Fork, Utah

Printed in the United States of America
First Printing: August 1996

01 00 99 98 97 96 95 94 10 9 8 7 6 5 4 3 2 1

ISBN 1-55503-985-5

Library of Congress Cataloging-in-Publication Data

Osguthorpe, Russell T.
        The education of the heart: spiritual foundations of teaching and learning/Russell T. Osguthorpe.
            p. cm.
        ISBN 1-55503-985-5
        1. Religious education--Philosophy.] I. Title.
BL42.074   1996
370'--dc20   96-26624
                                                                     CIP

PRAISE FOR

THE EDUCATION OF THE HEART
Rediscovering the Spiritual Roots of Learning

BY DR. RUSSELL T. OSGUTHORPE

By now, we in the West should understand the terrible price we pay for educating only the mind. Too many "educated" people possess the technical power to manipulate the external world but lack any sort of self-knowledge, ethical compass, or appreciation for the sacrament of life.

In *The Education of the Heart,* Russell Osguthorpe maps a new path for teaching and learning. Drawing on the ancient meaning of "heart"—not merely the seat of emotion, but the centerpoint of the human self where faith and intellect and emotion and will converge—Dr. Osguthorpe provides both theoretical foundation and practical implementation for the kind of education we need. His writing is rich with stories from experience, the wisdom of his religious tradition, and his own instincts as a gifted educator.

His book is a valuable contribution to a growing body of literature that shows us where education must go in the years ahead if it is to help heal a broken world.

—Parker J. Palmer,
Author, *To Know As We Are Known*

Russ Osguthorpe knows by virtue of the lived experience what constitutes an education of the heart. In this book he does a masterful job of leading the reader through the journey he has pursued as a result of his own interest in better understanding the nature of teaching and learning. *The Education of the Heart* deals with a topic that any teacher or learner needs to appreciate and grasp more fully. Few books can rival this one for a thorough and careful explication of the subject matter while, at the same time, providing such an enjoyable, uplifting experience for the reader.

—Robert S. Patterson, Dean
College of Education, Brigham Young University

We live in a period of profound changes in our civilization. There is nothing more central to our society than a solid education based on universal values; otherwise, sooner or later the human race is doomed to perish. *The Education of the Heart* presents a vision of reconstructing educational systems around the world on the basis of love. This is a leap in the right direction.

—Ryszard Pachociński
Institute for Educational Research
University of Warsaw, Poland

Russ Osguthorpe's book *The Education of the Heart* reveals the author's innate wisdom and love of his fellows, as well as his steadfast faith that has honed his teachings and continues to enrich his life and that of others. The reflections he offers to the reader are truly universal.

—Tom Russell, Professor
Faculty of Education, Queen's University
Kingston, Ontario, Canada

Reading *The Education of the Heart* prompted me to think differently and more deeply about learning and teaching, particularly my own learning and teaching. I am questioning, pondering, and searching in new dimensions.

—Charles B. Myers, Professor
Peabody College at Vanderbilt University

CONTENTS

ACKNOWLEDGMENTS

Although I have been writing professionally for many years, I have never felt so indebted to so many for their help and encouragement as I have while writing this book. When I first began thinking about the "education of the heart," I approached Arthur Henry King with the idea. Although we had known each other for fifteen years, I had never worked with him on a writing project. I will always be grateful for the way he welcomed me into his home and took a genuine interest in my work. Our "chats," which sometimes lasted for several hours, helped me in ways that go far beyond the writing of the book itself.

My present BYU associates also provided invaluable support and offered helpful suggestions throughout the writing process. Bob Patterson gave me the "space" to write the book and then continued to enrich the ideas in the book as it took shape. Beverly Cutler likewise supported the effort with her expressions of faith and encouragement, as well as with her keen editorial eye. With their typical unselfish competence, Sharon Black and Sheila Hewett also improved the manuscript by their careful reviews.

Some of my associates continually sent material that helped shape my thinking as I wrote the book. Jane Birch, Clark Webb, and Garr Cranney (shortly before his death) all contributed to the effort by sharing books, citations, and their own examples of commitment. Monte R. Swain provided a thoughtful review of an earlier version of the manuscript, and Tim Pelton offered helpful suggestions for improving one section of the book. Librarians Afton Minor and Tom Wright helped me find what I needed when I needed it. Their expertise and generosity reminded me of the librarian in the movie, *Lorenzo's Oil,* who became a collaborator in the search.

    I particularly thank my Canadian friends Tom Russell and Jan Carrick for their encouragement and editorial suggestions. In addition, I am grateful to Leslie Iura, a professional editor who offered early encouragement to publish the book, and to Valerie Holladay, who helped to refine the manuscript prior to publication. Finally, my gratitude goes to my family who gave me the content for the book and seemed to understand that the time I spent alone writing would only draw us closer together.

FOREWORD

In 1986 I published a collection of talks entitled, *The Abundance of the Heart* (see Matthew 12:34). I chose the word *heart* largely for the reasons that the author included it in the title of this book. If we examine how the word *heart* has been used in spoken language (for we can learn more about a word from common speech than we can in formal writing), we shall discover the richness of its meanings. One might say, for example, "Have a heart and give a poor man a drink," or "I hadn't the heart to tell him the bad news." In the first example, to "have a heart" means to be sympathetic—sensitive to the need of another person, but in the second, "to have the heart" means to have courage. Graham Greene once wrote a novel entitled, *The Heart of the Matter.* He used the term to indicate that his novel would treat the main point, the point of central importance. But he also used it, I believe, to indicate that the story would be emotionally charged. Thus we see that the word *heart* is used to convey messages of centrality, intensity, power, courage, and feelings.

Seeking the word *heart* in scripture, we find it alongside the words *mind* and *soul* (e.g., "Love the Lord thy God with all thy heart, and with all thy soul, and with all thy mind," Matthew 22:37). Some assume that because the three terms occur in succession that their meanings are different. I believe that such usage indicates intensity rather than differentiation of meaning. The remarkable aspect of these three terms is their similarity, the fact that they are interchangeable. Some mistakenly think that the word *mind* indicates only one's ability to think and that *heart* indicates only one's ability to feel. But thinking and feeling cannot be separated in a human being. One thinks and feels simultaneously, not in succession. All three terms, *heart, soul,* and *mind* refer to our wholeness as human beings, the oneness of our spirit and body. The book before you reminds the reader of the importance of this oneness in the teaching and learning processes, and at the same time points to the connection between what Faust called "word" and "deed." It is not enough to understand meaning—if one remains in the word, one is doomed. An individual's will must lead to proper conduct, to reliance on the Lord's power to assist one in doing what is right and good. Then there is no need to worry about the warning that a "little" power will lead to "unrighteous dominion" when we realize that it is not the amount of power that is important, but the source of that power (see D&C 121:39). Thus this book teaches that ethical conduct is the aim of education and that literacy and numeracy must be mastered in an atmosphere of trust in which the teacher and the student become self-forgetful, willing to submit to one another in love.

When I put together my own book, I was in essence concerned with my own experience of conversion. I believe that conversion is also the fundamental message of this book—that you cannot really teach properly until you have been converted because not until then will you have the self-forgetful, outgoing, unsentimental warmth of regard, which is the kind of love that there should be between teacher and learner. It is a process of the heart that leads to conversion and that continues to help after one has been converted. Conversion may include a primal experience but it also requires many repetitions; it is a process that never ends. Likewise, the education of the heart is a process that helps one to teach better, to learn more effectively, and it too is a process that never ends.

Arthur Henry King
Professor Emeritus
Brigham Young University
May 1996

Preface

One evening, while editing one of the chapters in this book, I asked my wife if she thought I should include "the story about the tree that used to be in our back yard—the one with the tree house the kids built." Just at that moment my nineteen-year-old daughter entered the room and buoyantly announced that, while sorting through her old things, she had found *The Friendship Tree,* "the book you wrote for me when I was nine years old." The story I had written was based upon a mixture of my children's experiences with the tree in our backyard and my own experiences as a child with a tree in my parents' yard.

I was prompted to write *The Friendship Tree* when some workmen drove their truck onto a field adjoining our property, grabbed their chain saw, and felled a large Chinese elm that had been a favorite place for my children to play. Because it was the only mature tree in our neighborhood, my children had chosen it as the spot for their tree house, an elaborate construction complete with an elevator operated with ropes and pulleys. They still enjoy talking about the tree and the time the elevator failed and my son plummeted to the ground. The evening before the dreaded "tree choppers" arrived, my children asked me to take their picture in the tree—just one last time. I got my camera and shot several frames of my children sitting in the tree with the sun setting in the background.

The tree has become a symbol for my children of their growing-up years. They cried when the tree came down, not only because it had provided a place for their tree house, but because it had provided, I believe, a place where they learned the lessons of life—lessons of creating, lessons of sharing, and lessons of love. As they talk about the tree today, they laugh about their experiences as they remember how things used to be.

When they were designing the tree house, they searched for scrap materials to construct the platform and the elevator. Only rarely did they ask that I go to the hardware store to purchase a needed part. They learned that they could design and build things on their own—or at least almost on their own—and that their creations could benefit not only themselves but their neighborhood friends as well. Their learning required their thought, their devotion, and their physical energy. They experienced success as well as frustration. And although they likely did not view constructing the tree house as learning at the time, I am certain that they consider it an important part of their learning as they reflect on it today.

When my nineteen-year-old daughter told me that she wanted to read *The Friendship Tree* again before she went to bed, I thought about how fitting it was that her "discovery" had helped me to write this preface. Her announcement reminded me of that tree and the way it had come to represent many aspects of the education of the heart for our own family.

Just as my family had prompted me to write the children's story, they also caused me to begin thinking about this book and then helped me write it by the way they are living their own lives. So, while I hope that others will find the book useful, my first desire is that my children will gain something from it and that they will be able to pass on whatever they gain to their children and to those who come after.

One of the main messages of the book is that our own learning really had no beginning and will have no end. Even those who do not believe in a premortal existence or in an after-life cannot deny that they have been influenced by countless people who came before them and that their own influence will extend to generations yet unborn. For this reason, education in its broadest sense is a concern for all of us—old and young alike—all of our lives. This type of education is not confined to the walls of a school, a church, or a home, although it can happen in all of these. It occurs wherever our search for truth leads us—even in a tree house.

My hope is that those who read the book will be able to sense some of what I have experienced while writing it, for I have been experiencing what I have been writing about. I have asked questions that mattered to me—questions that took hold of me and demanded answers. I have sought those answers in an environment of support and guidance. And I have sensed some of the rich and unexpected fruits that always come when one engages in such a search.

Russell T. Osguthorpe
1995

INTRODUCTION

If the only thing I were interested in was the find, I wouldn't have been in it this long. It's what you see on the road to a comet that is just as exciting as the comet itself.
David H. Levy, amateur astronomer

David H. Levy is one of the world's best-known astronomers, but he has never taken a formal course in astronomy or been paid for the time he spends gazing through a telescope at the night sky. To date, however, 21 comets have been named after him, and in 1994 he delivered more than 300 lectures on astronomy in some 150 towns and cities.

Mr. Levy began hunting comets in 1965 at the age of 17 but did not find his first comet until 19 years later, after spending 917 hours and 28 minutes in the search. During the next four years he spotted six more comets in his "back-yard observatory using a 16-inch telescope he calls 'Miranda.' [He] named it after the Shakespearean character who searched for new worlds" (see McDonald, 1995).

After finding his seventh comet on his own, he began working with two professional astronomers, Eugene and Carolyn Shoemaker. Together they have sighted an additional 14 comets. When Mr. Levy engages in a search for comets, his personal questions drive his efforts. When looking through the eyepiece of a telescope, "you never know what you're going to see," he says. "I'll go outside and I'll outline mentally an area of the sky that I want to study, and I think to myself, 'I wonder what I'm going to find in that area? Am I going to find a galaxy that I haven't seen before? A very red star? Or am I going to find a comet?' Whatever it is, it's going to be interesting. So just before searching, I feel like I'm looking at the sky and saying, 'O.K., sky, it's your show. Make my night.' And with that attitude, it's never failed to be an exciting time" (McDonald, 1995, p. A-12).

David Levy's experiences, and those of others like him, have helped me see learning in a new light, different from how I viewed it as a student, or even later as a teacher or as a parent. Like many others, I used to think of learning as what happens when a person reads a book, watches a PBS television program, or completes a school assignment. Basically I saw learning as a process of taking in "information" so I could recall it later to do something or say something I could not have done or said before I had learned the new piece of "information."

Many would not see my early definition of learning as seriously deficient. In fact, I can think of several education texts with definitions very close to mine. But there is something missing from this view of learning, and it cannot be corrected simply by adding a small piece to a nearly complete puzzle. The definition, I am convinced, is fundamentally incorrect.

Mr. Levy, for example, would probably not describe his comet hunting as a "learning experience." He might refer to it as his life's work, his hobby, his passion, but not his approach to learning. A closer examination of his story and others like it, however, reveals that learning—a more broadly defined, deeper kind of learning— was at the core of the experience from the beginning, and must remain, I believe, at the core for an individual or a group (a family, business, school, or church) to stay "alive."

The more I consider what learning is, the more I see it as a sacred privilege, an act of wonder. I believe that when we are learning we feel most alive—when we are learning, we feel closest to God. Why is it then that so many view learning as a form of drudgery, as something to be avoided? I recently read about an immigrant who had worked for Motorola in Chicago for over a decade. She spoke good English and was viewed by her supervisor as a competent contributor. But when the corporation invited her to participate in Motorola University's professional development courses, she was reluctant to attend, fearful that she might fail. Rather than being a sacred privilege, an act of wonder, learning for her represented something painful and punishing. Her story reminded me of the hesitancy and fear I used to see on the faces of many newly divorced single parents as they entered a program designed to help them with career planning. Their past experiences with formal learning had obviously not been positive.

I began examining David Levy's experience to see if I could identify what set it apart from the type of experiences that caused the immigrant worker or the single parents to have an aversion to learning. And as I considered the Levy story and compared it to other stories of this deeper kind of learning, I began to sense what was missing for these hesitant learners. But naming the missing piece was another matter. I knew it was something deeply human, something at our center, something that signified wholeness and at-one-ness. I came to see that *where* this learning occurred was not the critical point; it might occur in a home, in a school, or in a personal place that is specifically ours. It might occur publicly with other family members, co-workers, or classmates, or it might take place privately in a moment known only to the learner. I might have named it *the education of the soul,* because the soul encompasses the whole person—spirit as well as body. But I chose to call it *the education of the heart* because the word *heart* reminds us that our wholeness comes from our very center, and it is the heart, I believe, that we as parents, teachers, or friends often overlook when we are trying to help another person learn.

There was a time when people understood the meaning of the word *heart* and recognized its connection to learning. Like the word *soul,* the heart signified more than the human spirit or emotions: it referred to the individual's wholeness, a place of thought as well as feeling. Early prophets and philosophers taught that unless the heart was right, or "rectified"—unless a person could look at a new thing both spiritually and physically, with both feelings and thought—the new thing could not be understood because it could not be experienced appropriately (see Pound,

1951). When a parent rigidly demands that the youngster complete a homework assignment in biology rather than play in a championship volleyball tournament, an angry child may learn something about resentment but very little about biology. I like the words of Confucius as translated by Ezra Pound (1951):

> If there be a knife of resentment in the heart or enduring rancor, the mind will not attain precision; under suspicion and fear it will not form sound judgment, nor will it, dazzled by love's delight nor in sorrow and anxiety, come to precisions. If the heart have not stable root, eager for justice, one looks and sees not; listens and hears not; eats and knows not the flavors. (p. 5)

The heart, then, represents the human center, the center of feeling and being. If the heart is not "rectified," real learning—mental, physical, or spiritual—cannot occur. When learning becomes something to avoid—a kind of punishment—I believe it is because the learner's heart is not rectified. This may be what is meant when we say, "the person's heart is just not in it," meaning that although the person may be going through the motions, *pretending* to learn, learning is actually not occurring.

And we can feign learning for only so long. I think of an interview I had with two young women in their first semester at the university. When I asked them how things were going, the first shrugged her shoulders, tilted her head to the side, and said, "Well, it's *school;* it's just *school."* The other student smiled and said, "It's everything I hoped it would be; I love it." The longer we talked, the more I could see that one student's heart was "rectified" while the other's was not—one's heart was in it, and the other's heart was somewhere else.

I am not saying that the former student's reaction necessarily developed out of selfishness; she may have experienced education where her teachers' or parents' heart was as ill-placed as her own. If one of her teachers or parents had viewed learning as I did—the accumulation of "information" bits—her frustrations might be quite understandable. When those who teach adhere to this incomplete, warped view of learning, they risk developing similarly incomplete and warped views of teaching.

I have observed in myself and in others the temptation to view teaching as the dissemination of information—a process akin to the way a dictator tries to distribute "correct information" to citizens. The *China Daily* newspaper, for example, typically devotes the upper left-hand corner of its front page to a story about the phenomenal success of a government-sponsored farm program or business venture. But few Chinese citizens are fooled; few actually take in the "information" as the government intended. They have learned to ignore it—even when the "information" is accurate—because it carries no personal meaning for them.

Similarly, when a parent or teacher forces "information" on children, they often choose to ignore it the same way Chinese citizens ignore the *China Daily*. Children may remember the information for a test, but as soon as the test is over, they forget it because they do not believe it or cannot make it personally meaningful. Only when learning becomes personal, when the learner makes choices and the spirit and body unite, will learning find a lasting place in one's soul.

I have come to see this kind of learning as a form of repentance. When we repent of an undesirable behavior, we turn away from it and embrace a new way of behaving. When we truly learn, we also turn away from a former way of thinking and feeling and embrace a new way. Just as the sinner must first recognize the need to change, so the learner must sense the need to search for truth. In both instances, the act is intensely individual, but it requires assistance—from family members, teachers, and friends, as well as from God.

If we accept that there are deeper, more satisfying definitions for learning and teaching, where might we search for them? We might attempt to find these new definitions in current books and articles on teaching and learning. But while we will discover much to contemplate in this body of literature, we may not identify the secrets underlying the kind of learning David Levy experiences; we may not even be able to find words that embrace this more complete form of learning and teaching.

The desire to find such terms has led me to search for roots more than for branches. I want to rediscover the ideas we seem to have lost in teaching and learning, the ideas that our ancestors understood, the truths that Christ taught. These are the roots—the foundation—and we cannot understand where the new "branches" or definitions fit or how they relate to one another until we understand the sources from which they spring, until we trace their meaning back down the trunk to the roots. And if our "genealogical research" leads us to roots that are unhealthy or that grow in sandy soil (in other words, are based upon faulty assumptions), we must keep searching until we find those that are firmly planted in the soil of eternal truth.

Such terms would be older and richer than those in most current literature about education—words that have long been connecting us with each other and with God. These terms would describe the roots of teaching and learning, not just the branches—words like *faith, love, joy, reverence, discernment, and humility, or inspire, ponder, and edify.* These terms were once central to teaching and learning but have long since lost their place in our conversation about education. In this book I will attempt to restore them to their place.

The book is organized around three primary aspects of what I call the education of the heart: the question, the search, and the fruits. In the first section, I will discuss how a question of the heart lays claim on us as we lay claim on it, how it springs from the center of our being rather than being imposed on us, and how it arises out of a love for God and a love for others.

In the section entitled "The Search," I will explain how we must have faith as we begin our search, how we should "ponder in our heart" the truths we find, and how we can rely on guidance from God and others throughout our search.

In the final section I will describe the fruits of such a search.

These are not what we typically expect from teaching and learning. Rather than intellectual, social, or emotional results, they might be described as spiritual fruits—the qualities of knowing and being that grow inside us as we experience the education of the heart. This type of education causes students to become more *discerning*, have *reverence* for God and his creations, increase in *humility*, develop *sensibility*, draw upon *inspiration*, *edify* others, and experience real *joy*. These terms do not identify the subjects being learned; they are the fruits of learning any topic in a new way. These terms define the development of individual integrity; they represent qualities of character that are the ultimate but indirect fruits of the education of the heart.

The section entitled "Class Notes" contains additional information directed specifically at those who are presently involved in the formal classroom as teachers or students. These footnotes occur at points throughout the book when I felt a need to relate a topic to the literature on teaching and learning.

I will draw upon a variety of examples, such as the experiences of David Levy, as I explain how each term relates to the education of the heart. The examples come from my own experience as a father, son, or student—as well as from my experience as a teacher in the university or for the young people I serve in church assignments. I will also include stories that have come to my attention through conversation, books, or the media. Some of these examples have come through friends or family members who, as they have attempted to understand the education of the heart, have shared stories they have encountered to help refine the definition that emerges in this book. Like me, these "fellow travelers" have begun to question their long-held definitions of teaching and learning, and have allowed their questions to lead them to "see and hear and eat and know the flavors" of the fruits of the search.

I do not claim to have found all of what it means to educate the heart. Rather, I offer the ideas in the following chapters as aids to help readers begin thinking about learning and teaching in new ways—in a sense as a new lens through which we can look to conduct our own search for truth, just as David Levy makes his nightly searches for undiscovered matter in space. For I believe, as did Levy's mentor Leslie Peltier, that the search itself is what counts—

> To hunt a speck of moving haze may seem a strange pursuit, but even though we fail, the search is still rewarding, for in no better way can we come face to face, night after night, with such a wealth of riches. (Peltier, quoted by McDonald, 1995, p. A-12)

These lines meant so much to Levy at the age of seventeen that he committed them to memory—he "learned them by heart." And he can still recite the lines today—thirty years after he first read them. The lines remind us that we too can experience the joy of the search if we develop such commitment. And that when we are committed to the search for truth, the "riches" will come into view because our hearts will be "rectified." We will discover that even when we are not actively looking through the lens, even when we "sleep," our hearts will constantly "keep watch" (see Song of Solomon 5:2).

In his poem "Dreamtime," Gordon Personius explains how truth can distill upon us in the night—

> In the darkest halls of our nights
> many are the dreams that waft
> through the minds of all
> those who may know
> that sunlight
> dissolves
> all but those
> built out of truth
> the rest are like the night
> flowers blooming, then fallen
> but the senses remember the smells.
> (see Dumars, 1993, p. 25)

THE
QUESTION

CHAPTER ONE

QUESTIONS OF THE HEART

One sees what one carries in one's heart. (Goethe)
The creative soul recreates life
after the image he carries in his heart.
(Lowell Bennion, 1988, p. 56)

Most of us spend more time asking and responding to questions than we realize. Questions form the basis of good conversation. Some are relatively simple and require little thought, such as, "Do you need a ride home from school today?" Some are more complex and may confuse. But some questions seem to seek us out and take hold of us, questions we cannot ignore because they keep returning until we address them. They might be questions about whom we should marry, why a friend has cancer, or how we can help a child overcome depression. Unlike many of the questions we are required to answer, these questions are not found on the pages of a textbook, on a blackboard, or on a computer screen. They are not written on "tables of stone, but on the fleshy tables of the heart" (2 Corinthians 3:3).

LORENZO'S OIL

The true story of Lorenzo Odone (O dó nay), a six-year-old boy who had adrenoleukodystrophy (ALD), a rare and fatal genetic disease that afflicts young boys, illustrates the power of a question of the heart. Some may be familiar with the movie *Lorenzo's Oil*, which was based upon Lorenzo's parents' search for a cure.

As a young child, Lorenzo began to have accidents around the house and seemed to have difficulty at times controlling his arms and legs. When his parents, Augusto and Michaela Odone, took Lorenzo to see a physician, no problems could be identified. After a series of frustrating visits to medical centers, the Odones at last found a physician who diagnosed Lorenzo's disease as ALD, a disease that strips away the myelin—the insulating tissue that surrounds the nerve endings. There was no cure for the disease, the Odones were told; the medical profession was just beginning to understand what it was. A cure was simply not available.

The Odones knew that if they did not respond quickly, Lorenzo would die. Both Augusto and Michaela went to the library and began reading everything they could find on ALD. They learned that the disease makes it impossible for the body to digest fatty acids and that the rise in fatty acid levels gradually destroys not only the body's myelin but all of the vital organs. Thus, the Odones' search became more specific: "How can we lower Lorenzo's levels of fatty acids?"

After months of intensive study, they had the idea of using oleic acid, an extract from olive oil. They administered the oleic acid to Lorenzo but found that his fatty acids decreased only half as much as needed. To reach normal levels, Lorenzo's fatty acids needed to be reduced twice as much as they were with the oleic acid.

As Lorenzo's condition deteriorated, Augusto returned to the library, studying all the scientific literature he could find on long-chain fatty acids. When his research failed to yield what he was looking for, he sought help from others who were seeking a cure to ALD.

After months of research, Augusto hypothesized that an extract from rapeseed oil might effectively reduce Lorenzo's fatty acids to normal levels. Since the oil was not approved for human consumption in the U.S., no American firm would produce the substance. At last, Augusto located a chemist in England who, although ready to retire, agreed to extract the substance from rapeseed oil so that Augusto could try it with Lorenzo.

Lorenzo's condition had already deteriorated significantly by the time the Odones received the oil from the British chemist. Nevertheless, they tried the oil and found that it did indeed reduce Lorenzo's fatty acids to normal levels.

As I watched the story unfold, I found that I was thinking more about the Odones' experience as learners than I was about the intricacies of Lorenzo's disease or the details of the progress that Michaela and Augusto were making in their search for a cure. I thought about how seldom anyone is captured by a question the way the Odones were captured. As learners we often respond to questions that others impose upon us; at times we even ask our own questions that lead us to search for answers. But seldom do we ask with the intensity and commitment that I observed in these two parents attempting to save the life of their son. Their question, although it was technical, involved more than the intellect, more than the simple accumulation of bits of information. It was a question that sprang from the heart, a question that demanded their whole soul.

I wondered, "Can such questions arise only when we have a personal or a family crisis such as the Odones were experiencing? Must we wait for a life-threatening illness to learn with our heart—to apply our spirit, our intellect, and our physical energy in one united whole to a question?" I thought about the broader implications for learning that the Odones' example portrayed. I noticed, for example, that as Augusto and Michaela kept searching for a cure to their son's illness, others—such as the librarian— came to their aid in a natural, almost a preplanned way. I recognized examples in my own life of such assistance; faces came to my mind of others who had helped me in my own "searches"—my parents, my wife, my children, my teachers, and my church leaders—all of whom had taken an interest in me and had joined me in my search, just as the librarian had joined Augusto.

WHAT IS A QUESTION OF THE HEART?

I had experienced the kind of learning I had observed in the Odones, and I knew others who had experienced it. But I had never put a name to it; I had never thought about it long enough really to understand it. And as I kept wondering, I began to see the importance of *questioning* in this type of learning. Without the

Odones' original question, without their perplexity over Lorenzo's illness, they would never have engaged in such an intense search. Theirs was a question of the heart, one that engaged their whole being.

My observations of the Odones and others helped me to see that such questions spring from a desire to *be,* as well as from a desire to *know.* They originate in the center of our being. They are not imposed on us. They are based on real needs—needs we are uniquely meant to address. They arise out of love—a love for God and a love for others. Because of their inherent power, these questions lay claim on us (Palmer, 1993). They capture our attention, our energy, and our devotion. We cannot rest until we have obtained our answer.

We may not know what to call such questions, but we know they are different from the types of questions others ask us when they want to teach us something. Some might believe that such questions are limited to issues of morality or emotion. But although they arise out of love, questions of the heart can address any topic that requires the combination of intellectual, spiritual, and physical response—for they do not ignore the intellect. They are simply not restricted to the intellect alone. They are questions we alone can pursue. Other individuals may have similar questions—even some that appear to be identical with ours—but because they ask them and pursue them in their own unique way, their questions are theirs and ours are ours.

Questions of the heart grow deeper and stronger as we respond to them because the closer we come to truth, the more we are drawn into a search that takes hold of us and never lets go. Such a search always prompts us to do and say things that will edify others—never to put others down or draw attention to our own abilities or accomplishments. Questions of the heart inevitably draw us closer to God, the one who has always known and loved us.

Questions of the heart demand an investment—not only from the one who initially asks the question, but from others as well. The investment may take many forms: an investment of time, physical or spiritual energy, or even money. But the investment is always in response to God or to another person; it always comes by invitation rather than by compulsion. In the Odones' case, Augusto invited the response of the librarian and the chemist, and they responded. They invested themselves in the Odones' search, in Augusto and Michaela themselves, and eventually in Lorenzo—the one who gave rise to the initial question of the heart.

As I kept pondering the idea of questions of the heart, other examples emerged. The examples that meant most to me were those that had grown out of my own experience, my own learning from my childhood to the present. As I reread the stories most familiar to me, I began to understand things differently than I had in my youth—to appreciate old "friends" in new ways. One of these stories I had encountered in my early childhood—the account of Joseph Smith, who would become the founder of The Church of Jesus Christ of Latter-day Saints (LDS). As a young boy in upstate New York in 1820, Joseph Smith sought answers to his questions about God and religion. I had read the story and thought about the story all of my life, but I had never considered the account from the standpoint of learning. When I did, I began to see things I had never seen before.

A PROPHETIC QUESTION OF THE HEART

The experience of Joseph Smith begins with his frustration at not knowing which church he should join. As he had listened to different preachers arguing with one another over points of doctrine, he had become increasingly confused. In his own words, he recounts how this frustration and confusion led to a question of the heart:

> During this time of great excitement my mind was called up to serious reflection and great uneasiness. . . .
> In the midst of this war of words and tumult of opinions, I

often said to myself: What is to be done? Who of all these parties are right; or, are they all wrong together? If any one of them be right, which is it, and how shall I know it?

While I was laboring under the extreme difficulties caused by contests of these parties of religionists, I was one day reading the Epistle of James, first chapter and fifth verse, which reads: *"If any of you lack wisdom, let him ask of God, that giveth to all men liberally, and upbraideth not; and it shall be given him."*

Never did any passage of scripture come with more power to the heart of man that this did at this time to mine. It seemed to enter with great force into every feeling of my heart. I reflected on it again and again, knowing that if any person needed wisdom from God, I did; for how to act I did not know, and unless I could get more wisdom than I then had, I would never know; for the teachers of religion of the different sects understood the same passages of scripture so differently as to destroy all confidence in settling the question by an appeal to the Bible. ("Joseph Smith History," in *The Pearl of Great Price)*

Joseph Smith's question was a question of the heart, a question that he experienced with his whole soul. Joseph's "mind was called up to serious reflection," but the message of the scripture came with power to his heart, which embraces all facets of our being— the mind, the spirit, the body. Like Joseph we all yearn for answers, we all yearn for wholeness, we all ask questions that demand our individual response. And I assert that only when we ask such questions will our most important learning occur.

How do such questions arise? How do they develop? Joseph's experience suggests that they come from deep within us. They are not surface questions like those so many of us ask as students, teachers, friends, or parents. They are not contrived from some predetermined "objective" and are seldom stimulated by someone's trying to teach us something. They develop gradually like a fire that is lit from burning coals—first smoldering, then building to a searing flame that we cannot ignore.

Joseph Smith was confused by the conflicting messages he

heard; he wanted to know where he fit, which sect he should join, and he recognized that he himself would need to act to find an answer. We can approach the most fundamental questions, those of religion or philosophy, from a strictly intellectual standpoint, relying only upon logic, analysis, and synthesis. Or we can approach such questions without any such intellectual involvement, solely through the emotions. Joseph did neither. He engaged in a serious search. He read, he listened, he discussed. But he also pondered and prayed. Through it all he remained open to what he would need to do to obtain his answer.

As parents, teachers, or learners, we sometimes make the mistake of relying too much on the intellect alone, strangling the life out of the very topic we are trying to learn or teach and missing the beauty and wonder of the questions that lie all around us. But it is also possible to miss the beauty and wonder by relying too much on feeling, even rejecting whole disciplines (for example, the student who says, "I hate math," and when asked why, responds, "I don't know, I just hate it").

The point of this chapter is not that a question of the heart must develop before learning of any kind can occur. Both Joseph Smith and the Odones had already learned much that affected their questions. Neither is it the point that all questions of the heart are of the magnitude of those of Joseph or the Odones. Some questions of the heart are small and may appear to be relatively inconsequential, but if we approach learning and teaching with questions of the heart—no matter how small—we will eventually face questions of real significance to us as individuals. What appears to be a remote, obscure question at one time can eventually lead to responses of real consequence. We should be slow to judge the "relevance" of questions that take hold of us, but rather allow each question to lead us to its natural conclusion.

While working on an early draft of this book, a French phrase on a book cover caught my eye: *Je dors, mais mon coeur veille.* Literally the phrase means, "I sleep, but *my heart awakens.*" However, as I thought about it, I began to prefer the translation,

"I sleep, but my heart keeps watch." The words suggest that even though our mind may not be conscious of something, we can still be aware: if our heart is open, we are never separated from God. As I continued to write, I found that distilling some of the ideas I was studying helped me "[keep] watch, that [I] might be ready" when truth knocked (see Doctrine & Covenants 50:45).

Watchwords
• Questions of the heart draw us into a search for truth that has neither beginning nor end. Some questions will lead to clear and unmistakable answers; others will simply lead to other questions that extend the search.
• A search that looks only to books or to the human mind can never fully satisfy a question of the heart; we must eventually reach outward to others and upward to God.
• Our family members and friends—those who know us best—are often most prepared to help us in our search.
• Being captured by a question, as were the Odones and Joseph Smith, is a prerequisite to the education of the heart.
• Questions of the heart are unique to each person. Individuals pursue such questions in their own way, but in the process are always drawn closer to others and to God.
• Unlike most approaches to teaching, which impose questions upon the learner, the education of the heart suggests that questions emerge inside the learner, questions that bring with them their own innate demand for a response.
• As answers to questions of the heart are pursued, intellectual, spiritual, and physical responses combine together in the search. We must engage in the search withholding nothing, allowing others and God to fill the voids that would prevent us from finding truth.

As students we may have learned to follow instructions; we may have learned to get good grades; but we may never have been captured by a question as Joseph or the Odones were. Until we are so captured, our learning will be limited. Questions of the heart are not a process or technique, they are the essence of the education of the heart—the prerequisite to a higher form of learning that does not fit comfortably into any existing definitions of learning. We need to make a place for such questions in our homes, schools, and individual lives (see *Class Notes,* #1). Because such questions cannot be assigned, imposed, or forced on us, we must first reconsider the functions of freedom and love in learning.

CHAPTER TWO

FREEDOM AND LEARNING

Know the truth and the truth shall make you free. (John 8:32)
I am the way, the truth, and the life . . . (John 14:6)

In the previous chapter I discussed how questions of the heart emerge, capture us, and cause us to learn in ways that change us. Such questions can grow inside us only when we are free to choose what and how we will learn. If we are to be free, what is the role of the teacher? How do we as parents or teachers know when to allow young people to choose and when to choose for them?

One day a distraught mother called me to ask if I could tutor her son in reading. She described how her fourteen-year-old boy (I will call him Randy) had gone through every special reading program she could find but still could not read. She pleaded with me to help Randy learn to read.

The mother's description intimidated me. A student of education at the time, I was not an expert in remedial reading, much less in the type of serious dyslexia Randy appeared to have. I expressed my reservations but offered to tutor him privately for two weeks to see how he would respond.

I began our sessions by testing Randy. The results of the tests showed that he was above average in intelligence but was reading below the first-grade level. He even had difficulty naming the letters of the alphabet, struggling with some of the same letter reversals common to kindergarten and pre-kindergarten children. I had seen many children at various ages with reading problems, but I had never seen anyone with difficulties as severe as Randy's. When he looked at the word *that,* he was as likely to say, "it," or "this," as he was "that." His ability to comprehend material read to him was superb; understanding the meaning of a story meant everything to Randy, so his word substitutions always made rational sense, even though the words shared few common letters.

I began tutoring Randy on the most basic concepts of reading that I had taught to my own children before they entered school. To my surprise Randy responded extremely well. He clung to every phonetic rule I introduced (for example, in the word *bate* the "a" is long and "e" is silent) and even begged for more after he had learned all of the basic rules. He became quite skilled at sounding out words he had never seen before—which was essential because his ability to hold a word in memory was the least developed I had ever encountered.

I became intrigued with his inability to remember "sight" words (words that do not follow phonetic rules such as *was* or *were*) and asked him to describe to me what went on in his mind when he saw a word such as *was* or *were*. Without hesitation he responded, "Oh, I have a whole bunch of words come to mind all at the same time, and then I just pick one." I asked him how he decided which one to "pick." "Any word that makes sense—I guess that's what I do," he answered.

We kept working together for several months, sitting on the lawn outside the faculty offices, reviewing the basics and then reading more and more. Randy finally read an entire book on the fourth-grade level. It was the first book he had ever read in his life, and he was almost fifteen years old. Reading was never easy for Randy, but he went on to graduate from high school, obtain an associate degree in art and design from a community college, and serve a mission for the LDS church during which he learned sign language so he could work with people with hearing impairments.

I knew I had helped Randy to read, but did I help him develop his own questions of the heart? To what extent was Randy *free* to create his own questions? Was he being forced to learn to read against his will? As his tutor, should I have waited for him to suggest how he wanted to learn to read before I began tutoring him? Who was actually in control—Randy, his mother, or me?

The issues that arose as I tutored Randy are much like the challenges that arise in my home, in my church assignments, or in my place of work because in each of these different teaching situations, I face the same dilemma: how can I find a balance between the amount of direction I give and the amount of freedom I allow? I can be too directive with my children just as I could be too directive with Randy; but I can also be too permissive, too detached in ways that can cause my child, a student, or a fellow worker to believe that I am uninterested and don't care. I have wondered, "Would Randy's desire to learn to read be considered a question of the heart? Was it *his* question or was it his mother's?"

Because questions of the heart can take root only in a soul that is free, one might conclude that all education must be initiated by the learner—that teachers and parents must teach only on request. But questions of the heart cannot emerge unless the learner has already gained some knowledge—knowledge that has come from tradition, from the past—knowledge that has come by obeying authority and thus giving up at least some measure of what we consider to be personal freedom.

This is the paradox of freedom and learning: we cannot learn (we cannot find truth) unless we are free, but we cannot be free unless we first learn (we first find truth) by submitting to one who already knows what we are trying to learn (see *Class Notes, #2*). This paradox has been with us for a long time (Oelkers, 1991). The paradox demands that if we wish to consider the role of freedom in learning, we must first settle on a definition of truth. It requires that we answer both questions simultaneously: What is truth and what does it mean to be free?

WHAT IS TRUTH?

Defining truth has occupied philosophers for centuries. Some have concluded that truth should be considered fixed and immovable; others have argued that it is a target that shifts and changes and can be defined only in relative terms. While a careful examination of each approach may help us bring perspective to our own view of truth, I will turn to the New Testament for the Christian interpretation of truth, a definition that ties truth to God. Pilate's encounter with Christ, for example, clearly portrays the Christian belief about truth:

> Pilate therefore said unto him, Art thou a king then? Jesus answered, Thou sayest that I am a king. To this end was I born, and for this cause came I into the world, that I should bear witness unto the truth. Every one that is of the truth heareth my voice.
>
> Pilate saith unto him, What is truth? (John 18:37-38)

There is great irony in the exchange between Pilate and Christ. Pilate was conversing with the embodiment of all truth but failed to recognize it. When Christ asked Pilate earlier, "Sayest thou this thing of thyself, or did others tell it thee of me?" (John 18:34), he was attempting to help Pilate face his own beliefs, his own truth, rather than being a puppet of the people. But Pilate failed to understand. He never saw the truth because he never saw the Son of God, even though he was standing face to face with him. Pilate was still trying to "establish the facts" when in reality there was only one fact, and that fact could not be separated from the one who embodied it—that Jesus was the Christ.

On other occasions Christ said not only that he *brought* truth but that he *was* the truth. Parker Palmer (1993) shows the importance of this Christian belief in our conception of the education of the heart:

> Christian tradition understands truth to be embodied in personal terms, the terms of one who said, "I am the way, and the truth, and the life." Where conventional education deals with abstract and impersonal facts and theories, an education shaped by Christian spirituality draws us toward incarnate and personal truth. In this education we come to know the world not simply as an objectified system of empirical objects in logical connection with each other, but as an organic body of personal relations and responses, a living and evolving community of creativity and compassion. (p. 14-15)

WHAT DOES IT MEAN TO BE FREE?

I once heard a religious leader say, "When I think about the youth under my direction who get into trouble, it seems that they grew up in two types of homes—one where the parents were too strict, the other where the parents were too lenient." I would not want to infer from his remarks that if parents could just be better parents, there would be no problem children. But I do relate to the dilemma of how much freedom to give my own children. It is a question we face as parents daily: how can I teach my children obedience and still allow them to act for themselves rather than be "acted upon"? (2 Nephi 2:14).

The questions of freedom that parents face every day are not unlike the questions that we face in the workplace. We often perceive the person we work for to be either too controlling or too vague in the way they communicate expectations. I remember one department chair at the university where I work who came to the Dean's Office, of which I was a part.

"If you'll just tell us what to do," he said, "we'll do it." Accustomed to a more directive dean, the department chair wanted more precise instructions; he wanted the dean to make this particular decision for him. The dean responded, "This is your decision. I want you to discuss it with your faculty and then come back with a recommendation that we can consider." But I have also heard faculty complain that decision-making is too centralized, that they do not have enough say in what happens in the institution. In both cases, the issue is freedom: how much autonomy should we give to others, especially those we have been asked to lead?

We can all remember teachers who were either too directive or not directive enough. As a student in a workshop, I was once given a blank sheet of paper and asked to list the topics I wanted to study in the workshop. As I struggled to respond, I thought to myself, "If I knew what topics I wanted to study, I would not have enrolled in the workshop. I don't even know what my choices are. That's why I signed up." But the examples of teachers who exert too much control are even more prevalent. A student recently described to me how his science teacher told the students on the first day of class, "If you have any questions, I'd be happy to respond to them now, but this is the last time I'll be able to take questions because we just won't have time in the future—there's too much to cover, and there's too many of you."

Thus the issue of freedom is at the base of all learning. Forcing a mature person to learn often builds resentment in the learner and seldom results in any lasting positive benefit. Truth can enter us only when we are reconciled to God, only when we have opened ourselves, listened intently, and heard what can come in the still, quiet moments that are the hallmark of the education of the heart. It is at these moments that we know we are free because we have submitted ourselves to truth and felt its healing influence breathe new life into us.

FREEDOM TO LEARN, FREEDOM TO LIVE

If we are to be free to learn, we must feel safe in the places where learning occurs—our homes, our neighborhoods, and our schools. I do not need to cite a list of statistics to demonstrate that many of our schools and neighborhoods are unsafe. We see accounts daily in the news of drive-by shootings, domestic violence, students attacking teachers, or predatory adults abusing children. In a country that calls itself "the land of the free," we are afraid to walk the streets at night, particularly in certain parts of town.

Reacting to the increasing violence that occurs in homes, schools, and communities throughout the nation, President Bill Clinton said, "If learning is the key to full freedom in America, it must necessarily be true also that people must be free to learn." The shootings with reckless abandon and the chaos in families and communities have brought us to the point where, said the president, "Too many of our young people are no longer free to learn" (see O'Donnell, 1994, p. A1).

The kind of freedom President Clinton calls for is much more fundamental than the freedom to ask a question in a class or the freedom to make a decision in the workplace; it is a freedom from evil, a freedom to learn without fear of being harmed.

FREE TO CHOOSE TRUTH

An ancient prophet taught that a person's choices ultimately lead to life or death: "And they are free to choose liberty and eternal life, through the great Mediator of all men, or to choose captivity and death, according to the captivity and power of the devil" (2 Nephi 2:27). This prophet would not have been surprised at the violence that we now see in our schools and in our neighborhoods. He knew that disregard for others and for life itself is the ultimate end of the pathway leading away from God. He knew that the farther we separate ourselves from God, the less real freedom we have because when we deny our spiritual center, we deny our eternal nature. When we deny our eternal nature, we make choices out of selfishness; and the more selfish we become, the more we are held captive by our own instincts.

LDS Apostle Boyd K. Packer (1980) clearly explains the nature of our individual choices :

> It is the misapprehension of most people that if you are good, really good, at what you do, you will eventually be both widely known and well compensated. It is the understanding of almost everyone that success, to be complete, must include a generous portion of both fame and fortune as essential ingredients. We want our children and their children to know that the choice of life is not between fame and obscurity, nor is the choice between wealth and poverty. The choice is between good and evil, and that is a very different matter indeed. (p. 21)

It is a "different matter" because if we come to understand that every choice we make eventually leads us closer to good or closer to evil, we will choose in very different ways than if we think our choices will simply lead to more money in our pocket or more trophies on our shelf. Knowing that life's choices are between good and evil ties us inseparably to God, the embodiment of all that is good and all that is true.

When we worry about which parenting approach has the right amount of freedom in it or which teaching approach allows the student to choose appropriately, we are focusing on the wrong thing. If we want the children in our homes or the students in our schools to be good, we will need to be good ourselves. We will need to focus more on what it means to be good. We will need to pay more attention to the education of the heart.

WHAT DOES IT MEAN TO BE GOOD?

While listening to a news commentator explain the results of a murder trial, I heard the phrase "in today's moral climate." The commentator was referring to the increased attention that is being paid to matters of right and wrong. During the 1970s and 1980s sex was free and greed was good, but somehow during the 1990s our society is beginning to understand the price of neglecting morality. That concern has led to the development of new programs to help parents and teachers teach their children to be good.

Although some character education programs seem to be leading in the right direction, many are poorly designed and inappropriately grounded. In fact, most of the character education proponents have resorted to teaching moral education in much the same way as we teach mathematics or history. Martin Buber (1965), the well-known Jewish philosopher, described the dilemma of trying to teach character development. He explains the relative ease of teaching a student to get the right answer to a math problem and the challenge of teaching students not to envy, to bully, or to lie:

> I try to explain to my pupils that envy is despicable, and at once I feel that secret resistance of those who are poorer than their comrades. I try to explain that it is wicked to bully the weak, and at once I see a suppressed smile on the lips of the strong. I try to explain that lying destroys life, and something frightful happens: the worst habitual liar of the class produces

a brilliant essay on the destructive power of lying. I have made the fatal mistake of *giving instruction* in ethics, and what I said is accepted as current coin of knowledge; nothing of it is transformed into character-building substance. (p. 105)

Robert Coles (1993) tells a story about his own attempts to teach moral reasoning that have led him to the same conclusion as Buber. Coles describes how a former student, a Rhodes Scholar, returned to tell Coles that he was unhappy with the education he had received at Harvard. In Coles' words:

[The student] said, "Well, I've taken two courses in moral reasoning and I got A's in both of them."

So I said, "Congratulations, but I guess you've been getting A's in everything."

He said, "It really hurt to get A's in those courses."

I looked at him and said, "What do you mean?"

He said, "Well, I got the A's in the two courses in moral reasoning, but I'm not a very good person. . . . "

And I said, "Oh, we all have our downers every once in a while. We all feel kind of not so good about ourselves."

And he looked at me and he said, "Dr. Coles, when you can get two A's in courses called moral reasoning and you can do some of the things that I've done, you begin to wonder about those courses."

I said, "What have you done?" . . . He then started telling me about the way he behaved with his roommates and with his girlfriend. And after I had heard this, I thought to myself, "He's absolutely right about himself. . . ."

He [then] said, "It really matters to me that my mind can do such good work and that it doesn't connect with my conduct."

All I could do was thank the student. . . .

[He then asked] "Well, what are we going to do about this." And I said, "Our entire lives are to be given over not only to contemplating this irony, but working hard to undo it. And maybe that's what education is about."

That is what the education of the heart is all about. It is about integrating the scholarly with the spiritual—finding the unity that has always been inside us but has been obscured by a culture that has separated the analytic from the integrative, the head from the heart, and the spirit from the body. By dissecting ourselves into two halves—the spiritual and the intellectual—we, like Robert Coles' student, might perform well on the written tests that are graded and ultimately mean nothing, but fail miserably on the performance tests that are not graded and ultimately mean everything. The more we try to separate the way we *act* from the way we *think,* the more we become entrapped. The education of the heart unites feelings and thoughts, analysis and holism, and the body and the spirit. I call this unity the *soul.*

Coles' student answered questions on moral reasoning correctly but failed to understand that each time he responded (both on the test and to other people), he was not merely making choices *about* good or evil—as defined by some theorist—he was *approaching* good or evil. During the time he was taking the course on moral reasoning, he was likely much more concerned about his scholarship application and its grade-point-average requirements than he was about God or truth. And by misconstruing his freedom of choice—thinking that he was choosing between "fame and obscurity" or between "wealth and poverty," he drew himself away from God, away from good, and away from truth. He felt "free" to behave immorally, only to find later that he could not live with himself: his selfish behavior led him away into "captivity." What at one point appeared to him as acts of personal freedom eventually appeared as acts of sin, acts of evil. He yearned for unity in his *soul.*

In the education of the heart, freedom and truth are bound together. We cannot consider one without considering the other. When we recognize this unity, we discover that freedom has nothing to do with following our impulses—being free to do whatever feels good at the moment—but freedom actually means being free from the anguish that Coles' student was feeling. It is sin—the kind of sin Coles' student finally recognized—that limits our freedom. We can be free only when we repent of the sin. Had Coles' student sought guidance from the scriptures, he would have learned that his past mistakes could be forgiven if he would simply forsake his sins and place his faith in the one who suffered for us all:

> For the law of the Spirit of life in Christ Jesus hath made me free from the law of sin and death. (Romans 8:2)
>
> If the Son therefore shall make you free, ye shall be free indeed. (John 8:36)
>
> But now being made free from sin, and become servants to God, ye have your fruit unto holiness, and the end everlasting life. (Romans 6:22)

FREEDOM, TRUTH, AND QUESTIONS OF THE HEART

Questions of the heart emerge from a soul that is truly free; they point us toward truth, and lead us to virtue. This is why questions of the heart make learning a sacred privilege, regardless of the specific topic we are attempting to learn. When we are learning anything, we should learn in a way that will allow a question of the heart to emerge. Randy, the ninth-grade student who was learning to read, may never have articulated his question of the heart, but I am convinced that he had one. Had he been able to frame the question, it might have looked something like this: "How can I learn to read? And how will learning to read help me find truth?" He knew that his mother had a deep desire to help him learn to read. He also knew that his father had had difficulty with reading all of his life and that lack of reading ability had limited his father in certain ways.

I am convinced that Randy was not trying to learn to read so that he could be wealthy or famous; he was learning to read because he knew it was the *good* thing to do. He also knew that it was his choice to learn to read. His mother, although she deeply desired to help Randy, never forced him to participate in the tutoring. He knew that at any moment he could discontinue the tutoring sessions. But he did not discontinue. His question of the heart drove him to invest his all in what was a painfully difficult exercise, but one that eventually bore fruit. And the fruit allowed Randy to be of greater service to others, to recognize truth, and to draw closer to God.

Robert Coles' student also had a question of the heart, one that sprang at least in part from a feeling of guilt. It was a very different question than Randy's, but still a question of the heart. Randy was learning, I believe, so that he could put his gifts and talents "at the disposal of the human race," while Coles' student may have been learning so that he could "put the human race at [his] disposal" (Nibley, 1989, p. 51). It was his realization of this incongruity that caused Coles' student to return to his professor for counsel. While he was enrolled in Coles' course, the student was exercising his freedom to choose, but his choices were focused on the wrong ends, and no written test in a course on moral reasoning could detect those ends; the ends were not even apparent to the student himself. Determining ends is always a matter of the heart, and this student had not yet involved his heart in his education—not until his question took hold of him.

Coles' student was not accustomed to being puzzled. And even though he was accustomed to having the right answers on tests, he was not accustomed to seeking truth. Even the course on moral reasoning likely separated seeking truth from seeking God, and thus, students found something other than truth. Only after sustained reflection did the student begin to seek truth. Only when he returned to Coles in a state of perplexity (see Dillon, 1988), did he begin to seek truth for the right reasons. Only then did a question of the heart emerge. Only then did the student begin to free himself from his perplexity and guilt.

Both Coles' student and Randy exemplify the relationship of freedom and truth to questions of the heart. Although Jacques Maritain, a French philosopher, did not use the term *question of the heart,* he described well how such questions lead us to God:

The fundamental orientation of man towards God is expressed each time that he performs a free act in conformity with right reason, each time that he chooses the good: "Now, when a man deliberating about his life chooses to love that which is good in itself, the bonum honestum, in order to link his life to it, it is toward God whether he knows it or not, that he turns himself." (In Allard, 1982, p. 41-42)

Thus, questions of the heart always lead to truth, to God; they liberate us not only from the tyranny of ignorance, but from the captivity of sin. They are questions that can shape our lives because they connect us to the eternal. The more we approach the question—the more we struggle for an answer—the closer we come to God and the more we come to realize our unique purpose and mission. And the more we understand our mission in life, the freer we become. As Maritain so eloquently explains, God's freedom becomes our freedom:

In a certain sense, this freedom makes us into gods. . . . There is in human freedom a participated similitude of divine, thanks to which, without being able to create anything properly speaking, we, however, as we please, cause that to be which was not and also form ourselves; thanks to which we are persons and, like gods, intervene in the order of the world by acts of endless scope; so much so that the mystery of our *activity* is as marvelous and as terrifying for whoever can be conscious of it, as the very mystery of our being. (In Allard, 1982, p. 31)

Watchwords
• The only way to overcome the paradox between truth and freedom is to tie ourselves and our learning to God. We do this by recognizing that any time we seek truth, we also seek God.
• The only way to expand our personal freedom is to deepen our commitment to truth.
• The most important kind of freedom is freedom from sin, free-

dom from enslavement to our unrighteous impulses. The only way to obtain such freedom is to recognize that all of our personal choices are ultimately choices between good and evil and then, after such recognition, submit ourselves completely to God.

• The way to free ourselves from the fear of violence and of inhumanity that is so prevalent is through the education of the heart.

• Questions of the heart lead us to truth and hence to greater freedom. Such questions are prerequisite to the education of the heart.

• Questions of the heart always have a moral dimension regardless of the topic being addressed.

Because seeking truth is an experience of intimacy, I will next discuss the relationship between questions of the heart and love. Love plays a central role in the education of the heart, one that is quite different from the role it plays in our present conception of education. Questions of the heart are not confined to boundaries of time or topic. They can occur in childhood, in youth, in adulthood, or in old age. But when they do occur, they will grow out of love—which always grows out of the kind of freedom discussed in this chapter.

CHAPTER THREE

LOVE AND LEARNING

The paths of freedom are those of truth and love. (Allard, 1988, p. 112)

There will be no metal detectors in this school; the only detectors we will have will be detectors of love. (John Pannell, Principal, Malcolm X Elementary School, Washington, D.C., in Gup, 1992)

Essayist and poet Wendell Berry (1989) tells about an experience in his childhood when he acted out of love toward his friend Nick, an African-American servant who lived and worked on Berry's Kentucky farm. Nick was Berry's friend, one who took him camping and fishing. Because Nick was black, he could not, therefore, be invited to Wendell's birthday party; but Wendell sent Nick an invitation anyway. Wanting to be kind to Wendell, but also needing to adhere to the social rules of the time, Nick decided to quit work early and come and sit "on the cellar wall." In Berry's words:

> By that time even I had begun to sense the uneasiness I had created: I had done a thing more powerful than I could have imagined at the time; I had scratched the wound of racism, and all of us, our heads beclouded in the social dream that all was well, were feeling the pain. It was suddenly evident to me that Nick neither would nor could come into the house and be a member of the party. My grandmother, to her credit, allowed me to follow my instincts in dealing with the situation, and I did. I went out and spent the time of the party sitting on the cellar wall with Nick.
>
> It was obviously the only decent thing I could have done; if I had thought of it in moral terms I would have had to see it as my duty. But I didn't. I didn't think of it in moral terms at

all. I did simply what I *preferred* to do. If Nick had no place at my party, then I would have no place there either; my place would be where he was. The cellar wall became the place of a definitive enactment of our friendship, in which by the grace of a child's honesty and man's simple-hearted generosity, we transcended our appointed roles. I like the thought of the two of us sitting out there in the sunny afternoon, eating ice cream and cake, with all my family and my presents in there in the house without me. I was full of a sense of loyalty and love that clarified me to myself as nothing ever had before. It was a time I would like to live again. (p. 53)

It was a time Berry wanted to recapture because it was a time, I believe, when he experienced his own education of the heart. He discovered something inside himself that he hadn't known was there, and he had acted on it. He was learning what we all must learn: to want to do what we ought to do. Although he could not have articulated it at the time, his question of the heart centered on the whys of racism, and when he "scratched the surface" he began to answer his own question, at least in part. If the rules of racism meant that Nick could not come inside, then Berry would go outside to be with him. An even more powerful lesson we learn from Berry's account is that this same question continued to fester in him, so much so that it led him to write the book in which he recounts the story of Nick and the birthday party. It is a book that was written, I believe, not out of duty but out of love for the black servants who played such an important role in his childhood.

When we act out of love freely, without coercion and without fear, we not only draw closer to one another, but we draw closer to God. The Odones experienced this when they began their search for a cure to Lorenzo's disease. Joseph Smith experienced it when he asked God for wisdom. And Wendell Berry experienced it when he decided to go outside by the cellar wall and sit with Nick. It is during these kinds of experiences that we learn our most important lessons about who we are and who we might become.

Just as the heart is the center of truth and of personal freedom, it is also the "seat of love." It is the heart that "keeps watch" and that is "awakened" when someone comes face to face with us, as Nick did with Berry, because it is in the heart that love resides (see Lévinas, 1993a).

FAMILY, LOVE, AND LEARNING

My wife's father is an inventor by nature. He is always creating some new gadget, tool, or device that will make life easier. He even designed his own home with the help of a drafting specialist, complete with a collapsible kitchen table and special blinds to help block out direct sunlight. But my favorite of all of his inventions is his now famous bread mixer. No, it is not the latest type that mixes and bakes the bread all in one easy step; it simply mixes the dough before it is placed in the bread tins and baked. The remarkable characteristic of the mixer is its price: only $20 (and that includes a $5 profit that he donates to the grandchild who sells it).

The idea for the invention came to my father-in-law about twenty years ago when his wife asked him to buy her a bread mixer. When he saw that the item cost over $100, he told her that he would see if he could "rig something up." He began immediately to tinker in his garage with whatever was close at hand. He found an old ice cream maker and concluded that if its motor was powerful enough to mix ice cream, it would be adequate to mix bread. All he needed was to find some sort of bread hook that he could attach to the ice cream motor.

After becoming dissatisfied with a bread hook he had made from steel, he successfully constructed one from aluminum. Threading one end of the hook, he then inserted it through a hole in a two-by-four he had cut to the length of the bucket opening, and secured it with a nut and washer. When he placed the two-by-four holder on top of the "bread bucket," he designed a wooden clasp with hinges so that the holder would remain tight on the bucket. His biggest challenge was locating the right type of bush-ing to surround the hook in the hole through the wooden holder. He spent approximately one year searching for a bushing that was strong enough and did not require any lubricant. A sturdy white nylon bushing was finally selected.

Once he had located all of the right materials and had per-fected the design (which required many formative tests), he was ready for production. While visiting him one summer day, I saw him in his garage with a stack of two-by-fours on one side and floor-to-ceiling stacks of finished holders on the other side. He was at that moment in the process of bending the hooks to place in the holders. The mixers were now ready for marketing.

A believer in the old-fashioned value of hard work, he offered to give $5 per mixer to any grandchild who wanted to sell them. In addition, he advertised in a magazine, which resulted in his mailing hundreds of the products to all parts of the country. We were one of the first recipients of his creativity, and we are still using the mixer after twenty years.

My father-in-law learned more than he ever expected about designing, producing, advertising, and preparing a new product. At one point he even contacted Proctor-Silex, the manufacturer of the original ice cream freezer, to determine their interest in mar-keting the mixer attachment, but while the idea intrigued them, the company had to decline because of changes it was making in its own product line.

What began as a response to a wife's request eventually bene-fited all of my father-in-law's family—either because they used the mixer attachment in their own homes or because they received funds for their education by selling the product. My father-in-law's learning grew out of love for his family. He did not enroll in any business courses at the local college; he did not even need to spend countless hours in the library as the Odones were required to do. His "teachers" were the hardware store owners who helped him find the right bushing, the magazine editors who helped him craft an effective advertisement, and most importantly his own wife who had caused him to initiate the project in the first place. She was his first and most significant critic. Not until she said that the machine worked could he feel satisfied that he had succeeded.

My father-in-law did not intentionally set out to "learn" something. He faced a problem—a need—and responded to it. But the problem did not emerge in an abstract way; the problem had a name and a face—it came naturally from one close to him, his wife. He simply could not ignore the request of the one he loved, and his response led him to investigate new things in new ways—all so he could provide what his wife needed.

THANKSGIVING IN PARIS

Thanksgiving has always been one of my favorite holidays; it is one holiday that has escaped much of the commercialism that surrounds most others, a holiday that still "remembers" its roots, one that is still practiced much as it was centuries ago. It is an American holiday, one that few other nations have adopted. I have enjoyed celebrating the holiday since I was a young boy, but my most memorable Thanksgiving occurred in 1994 in Paris. Three of my children, my wife, and I spent August through December of 1994 in France so that I could study the French system of education and they could experience another culture.

About two weeks before the holiday, my wife told me that she wanted to invite some friends to our apartment to share Thanksgiving dinner with us. I looked back at my wife and said, "Are you sure you want to invite a lot of people? We don't have the right pans to cook the turkey in; we don't have the right ingredients to make the kinds of foods we're used to. Are you sure you want to try to do this?" She looked back and said, "I really want to do it. I want to have the missionaries come, and I want to invite the friends we've met here—they've been so good to us."

We quickly learned that turkey buying in France is different than in the U.S. In France you must *commander* (order) your turkey at least two weeks in advance. So my wife went immediately to the store in our apartment complex to place an order. The

butcher told her that it was too soon to *commander* the turkey—
Christmas was still over one month away. She told him that she
needed the turkey in November; he told her that he would try to
get one.

During the next week, my wife began a serious "study" of how
to imitate American recipes in a place that does not have
American ingredients. She wanted most of all to be able to make
fresh rolls. Knowing that the flour was different, she decided to
try a few experimental batches.

However, the first batch of rolls did not taste quite right.
Something was wrong with the way the yeast was working; not
only did the rolls not rise as they should, but the taste of the yeast
seemed too strong. Every day the family welcomed another batch
of rolls—each time with a different kind of flour and a different
amount of yeast. Then one of the missionaries, who had studied
cooking in France when he was sixteen years old, told my wife
that she needed to buy *fresh* yeast from one of the local *patisseries*
(bakeries) and salted butter from the supermarket.

After much searching, I finally found a *patisserie* that had fresh
yeast and could sell it to me. My wife tried one more experimental batch of rolls and found that the fresh yeast and salted butter
indeed made the difference. My children were pleased that the latest recipe had succeeded but disappointed that the "experimentation phase" was ending.

The invitations went out, the menu started taking shape, and
I visited several more *patisseries* stocking up on fresh yeast. On the
Monday before Thanksgiving, my wife asked that I accompany
her to the store so that we could make certain that the order had
been placed. The butcher remembered my wife's request, went
into the back room to talk to his supervisor, and returned to tell
us that "my supervisor said that it's too early to order a turkey;
Christmas is over a month away." We are still uncertain about the
reason for the butcher's response. As the French say, our request
did not seem to "interest" him. Whatever the reason, it was dis-
couraging news. All we could think about was the advice that

French people had given us: "Make sure you order the turkey in plenty of time, because it takes quite a while to get one this time of year."

There was one more possibility in our small shopping plaza— a meat shop that was just large enough for four customers, the owner, and the meat. When I explained our problem, the owner acted as if he had known us for years. He responded, "I can get turkeys here by Wednesday afternoon. Will you need one or two?" We told him that we'd better *commander* two. "Do you want us to clean them, or will you do that yourself?" he asked. It was at this moment I began to wonder about my ability to understand his French. He continued, "Well, do you have a torch to burn the quills off, or would you rather have us do it?"

"Torch? Quills?" I responded. Even with the twenty-two pieces of luggage that we had hauled to France, we definitely had not had the forethought to pack a torch.

"So you would like me to clean them?" he asked.

"That would be great," we said, relieved that we would not be sitting around on Thanksgiving Day removing pin feathers by hand.

Finally, he even offered to cook them for us, "I could also cook the turkeys for you at no extra cost. If your dinner is at six o'clock in the evening, I could begin cooking them at three o'clock that afternoon, and you could come and pick them up at five o'clock." Now here was a tempting offer—"take-out-turkey"—why had Americans not thought of it? But how could he cook two twenty-pound turkeys in only two hours? we wondered. Was it all part of the "torching?" However, my wife convinced me that we should cook our own Thanksgiving turkeys, even though we had only one very small oven.

Upon returning to our apartment I suggested that we ask one of our French neighbors if we could use her oven on Thanksgiving Day. Although we felt awkward making the request, Madame Troussard graciously offered us the use of her oven.

On Thursday morning we walked over to the meat shop to

pick up the turkeys. Recognizing us immediately, the butcher said, "Your turkeys arrived, and they are some of the biggest and best ones I've ever seen." But they still had quills poking out with some of the pin feathers still attached. He got his torch and began to "clean" them, all the while explaining that the torch helped to sear the skin so that all the juices stayed in during cooking.

After hefting the birds back to our apartment we prepared them for cooking. I volunteered to cook the turkey in the Troussard oven while my wife watched over the one in ours. I placed the turkey in the Troussards' pan and, *guessing* which centigrade temperature to select on the dial, I inserted the turkey in the oven and went back to our apartment. About twenty minutes later, I returned to check on the turkey. I knew I was in trouble when I "heard" it cooking as soon as I opened the apartment door. I opened the oven to see it crackling and popping, grease spattering everywhere. It was cooking much faster than I had anticipated. "This must be a convection oven," I thought. The outer skin was turning brown after only twenty minutes.

After I reduced the temperature on the Troussard turkey, both turkeys finished cooking at about the same time, just before the guests arrived. Because the invitation list had kept growing, we had a full house. The evening turned out to be our favorite memory of our time in Paris. Watching my wife pull the hot rolls out of the oven, I was reminded of the movie *Babette's Feast,* the story of a woman who devoted all of her "inheritance" to a single, gourmet meal for the townspeople. This was my wife's way of giving back what she felt so many had given her—not only during our stay in France, but during her entire life. The guests stayed long after the meal ended. We talked and sang and talked some more.

In the process of preparing the dinner, we had all learned a lot. Our most important lesson, however, came not in our new-found knowledge about yeast, convection ovens, or French turkeys. What we learned most was the connection between love and learning. Just as love for their son had led the Odones to seek a cure, and just as love had led Berry to sit with Nick during his birthday party, love for our friends in Paris had led my wife to prepare a Thanksgiving dinner.

When we begin to see the connection between love and learning, the old, more narrow definitions of learning seem hollow and sterile. When learning grows out of love, everyone is changed for the better, but only if we understand the meaning of the word love.

WHAT IS LOVE?

Arthur Henry King (1986) has said:

> It is one of my strongest convictions that all love is ultimately one, in the sense that all love partakes of divine love, no matter how twisted and perturbed it may be. It is curious that Freud, too, should have thought that all love is ultimately one. Of course, he thought the one love was ultimately sexual. But we don't have to interpret that down. We can interpret it up. There ought to be a physical element in everybody's affection. We ought to be able to put a hand on the shoulder or waist of a fellow female or fellow male without people raising their eyebrows. I am not one who believes in the separateness of agape and eros. I believe . . . in the oneness of spirit and body in soul, [that] there is one love, and it is divine in all its forms. (p. 82)

Thus all love partakes of the divine because our spirit and body (our heart and our mind) make up our soul, which is whole and united. The more we "interpret it up," the more we connect ourselves to God. Our love, therefore, has nothing to do with self-actualization, self-esteem, or self-love. It is other-oriented and self-forgetful. It allows us to anchor our learning in the divine because we have made a place for Christ in our hearts: "That Christ may dwell in your hearts by faith; that ye, being rooted and grounded in love, may be able to comprehend with all saints what is the breadth, and length, and depth, and height; and to know the love of Christ, which passeth knowledge. . . ." (Ephesians 3:17-18).

Our definition of love is inexorably tied to our definition of truth and of freedom. Only when we are truly free can we express love that is complete because love that is tied to God must be freely given just as his love is freely given to us. Thus the education of the heart leads us to truth, which leads us to freedom, which leads us to love. Questions of the heart are thus born out of love.

Allard (1982), quoting Jacques Maritain, reminds us of the relationship between love and the search for truth and freedom:

> It is ultimately in God that the human person must seek to actualize his freedom of perfection; his freedom as his perfection become at once a conquest of man and a gift from God. Sanctity then becomes the personal ideal to be realized; in this state of perfection, terminal freedom coincides with the plenitude and the perfection of love, the love of God and the love of [others]. (p. 41)

WHAT OR WHOM SHOULD WE LOVE?

Maritain's conception of love coincides with sacred text, which is clear on how we should direct our love: we are to love one another and love God. We are counseled to "love truth" and "love *in* truth," and as discussed in the previous chapter, loving truth is akin to loving God (see 2 Nephi 9:40; 1 Peter 1:22; 1 John 3:18; 2 Thessalonians 2:10; *Teachings of the Prophet Joseph Smith,* p. 80). Love of ideas, love of topics, or love of learning for their own sakes are never mentioned in scripture.

We are specifically counseled to avoid directing our *love* toward the material things of the world: "For the love of money is the root of all evil" (1 Timothy 6:10) and "Love not the world, neither the things [that are] in the world" (1 John 2:15). My father-in-law loved neither the bread mixer he had invented nor the money that the product generated. He loved the people (his wife, grandchildren, and others) whom the invention could benefit. The cellar wall reminded Berry of his love for Nick, and I'm sure that the bread mixer reminded my father-in-law of his love for his family, but the physical symbols did not become objects of love themselves.

If we are to love one another and God, what about God's creations—is there a place for these in the education of heart? In so many ways his creations are everyday evidence to us that God exists and that he loves us. Scientists speak of the wonder and the oneness they experience with the plants and animals they study. Philosophers, such as Martin Buber, also describe unique relationships with trees and leaves (see Berry, 1985, pp. 1-38). Berry (1985) quotes Nan Hirleman as she caught herself "trying to 'get into the leaf'" so that she could understand it more fully (p. 20).

Hirleman's statement reminded me of an experience of a friend of mine—a faculty member in the Department of Botany. He developed an affinity for water-pollinated plants, and then one day on his way to work, he spotted one of these rare plants in the canal that he passed by every day. In his words—

> I glanced toward the canal and there it was—*Zannichellia palustris!* I couldn't believe it. Now imagine the scene. It's early morning. Students are scurrying to class along the sidewalk . . . and suddenly, with an excited look on his face, [a professor] rips off his sports coat, rolls up his trouser legs and jumps into the ditch! He reaches down, pulls up a small water weed, and closely examines it with delight. . . .
>
> Within an hour, I had brought tripods and high-speed cameras to the canal to study pollination. . . . We sent a description of [our study] to the world's expert on aquatic plants, C.D.K. Cook at the University of Zurich. His group repeated our study in Switzerland, and together with our respective students we published an announcement of our findings (Cox, 1995, p. 1).

My botanist friend would not have seen the rare plant in the canal had he not developed a love for such plants. Previous study had helped him to see for the first time what he had looked at many times before but had never really seen. For him these plants had become more than specimens; they had become manifestations of God's goodness and love for his children.

I am not a botanist, but I had an encounter a number of years ago with a colleague who taught me something about love and learning. As I was exiting the college building one evening, I saw the professor standing under a tree, waiting for his ride. He was about 50 years old at the time, but he appeared to be much older because (as I learned later) he was suffering from black-lung disease, which he had contracted in his youth while working in the mines of New Zealand. We had not spent much time together as faculty, but he motioned for me to join him under the locust tree that graced the entrance to the college. As I reached him he began talking about the beauty of the tree whose branches shaded us. Looking at me as if he had been my long-term mentor, he said, "You know, we have a relationship with this tree. This tree will be here long after we die. I know you can understand how we can have a relationship with this tree."

I wasn't sure that I fully understood at the moment what this good man was teaching me. But I do know that the tree took on new meaning, every time I exited the building. And then, not long after our encounter, the one who had introduced me to the tree died a premature death; his lung capacity gradually diminished until he could no longer take in oxygen, even artificial oxygen from a tank.

Not until after his death did I come to understand how he felt about that tree—a tree that produced the oxygen that he needed to sustain his life, oxygen that his lungs had such difficulty absorbing. It was a brief encounter for me that day but one that drew me closer to God and his purposes. Yes, there is a place in the education of the heart for the love of God's creations because his creations can connect us to each other and draw us closer to him. It is not insignificant that my experience with the tree was actually an experience with another person.

Questions of the heart grow out of love, and the love continues to grow when we seek answers to our questions. Teachers and learners alike (and we are constantly alternating in these roles) ask questions of the heart out of love, and they experience an increase of love when they pursue their answers. I am convinced that my friend who taught me about the tree knew and felt more after our conversation than he did before, as did I.

LOVE OF LEARNING

Many parents and teachers become confused and believe that learning itself is a thing to be loved, but we must remember that the love of learning for learning's sake is not our ultimate goal. Directing our love in this way can even separate us from other people and from God, rather than drawing us closer together.

> But what is more precious than the knowledge that we are individuals of infinite worth, having free agency? That is what love starts from. To have love, there must be some sense of the individual; there must be individuals to love and be loved. We can't really love ideas; we can't love abstract notions. We are made to love individuals. (King, 1986, p. 23)

As parents and teachers we want our children to be so attracted to a topic that they will want to learn more about it. We worry that we may even cause them to hate the topic we are trying to teach them. But when someone dislikes a topic, or an entire discipline, it is because the person does not understand how it fits into truth, how it is necessary to the person and those the person loves, and how it connects the person to God. It is this kind of understanding that we need to seek in our teaching and in our learning. Then we, as either teachers or learners, will be directing our love in ways that not only will help us enjoy the topic we are learning but will result in an increase of love toward others.

OBJECTIVITY, LEARNING, AND LOVE

Some might worry that bringing love into education will hinder learning because the one teaching will begin to coddle students, reducing rigor and objectivity. Not so. On the contrary, whether the learning is between student and teacher, parent and child, or administrator and employee, the love that unifies us in the education of the heart increases our ability to find truth. It helps us to see "things as they really are . . . and as they really will be" (Jacob 4:13). Only through love can our eyes be opened to the future, to the potential that lies within those who stand by us as we teach and as we learn.

LOVE OF LEARNING AND LOVE OF MONEY

Learning more does not mean that we will be happier, more fulfilled human beings, nor does it mean that we will live more moral lives. We might be content with our professional title, our salary, our material possessions, but then we are in danger of becoming "content with contentment" (King, 1986, p. 27). We have learned; we have even loved learning; but we have never understood its real purpose—to bring us closer to truth, to God, and to others. This explains why learning does not necessarily lead to a better life and why it is possible to be learned but never experience the education of the heart.

The purpose of learning is to identify and develop our talents and gifts so that we can assist others. But we must be careful in the process; we must constantly "keep watch" to ensure that our motives are indeed pure.

> We may ask for some gifts, as they are given, *without measure,* without limit; with others enough is enough, as Paul tells us (see 2 Corinthians 10:13). The *unlimited* gift that God's children from Adam on have been encouraged to seek with unceasing zeal is of course light and truth. . . . Selfish? The greatest pleasure in having knowledge is to spread it around. (Nibley, 1989, p. 142).

Rather than drawing a line between seeking the material

goods of the world (those things for which "enough is enough") and seeking truth (which we may ask for "without limit"), we have allowed the love of money and the love of learning to become dangerously entangled. Opportunities for formal education—even among the young—are frequently related to money in the form of tuition. And following graduation we often have difficulty ignoring the connection between knowledge and money when our promotions and salary are tied to learning throughout our careers.

The education of the heart draws us closer to God and away from materialism, or the attachment to things *of* the world (Joseph Smith Translation, see 1 John 2:15). It does not foster in us a feeling of "contentment" or complacent satisfaction with our present condition. Rather, it creates in us a sense of "divine discontent," a thirst for the living water that the Savior gives us freely (see Maxwell, 1976, p. 29). It puts a premium on love and relationships, and pays no heed to prosperity. It brings hope and prompts us to pray, as Thomas a Kempis (1340-1471) did centuries ago, that our heart will always bear the name of the Lord:

> Write Thy Blessed Name, O Lord Upon My Heart.
> There to remain so indelibly engraved
> that no prosperity or adversity
> shall ever remove me from thy love.
> Be to me a strong tower of defense,
> a comforter in tribulation,
> a deliverer in distress,
> and a faithful guide to the courts of heaven
> through the many temptations
> and dangers of this life.
> O Jesu, my only Savior!
> Write thy blessed name, O Lord, upon my heart.

Watchwords
• Love is born out of true personal freedom. Only when we enjoy God's freedom can we experience God's love. And because this kind of freedom is inseparably tied to seeking truth, so love is inseparably tied to the education of the heart.
• The education of the heart is a selfless, other-centered form of learning and teaching because questions of the heart spring from a love for others and for God. Just as seeking truth is prerequisite to the education of the heart, so is a love for others and for God.
• The education of the heart not only is based upon love, but it results in an increase of love in both the learner and the teacher. When we are seeking answers to questions of the heart, our love for those who assist us and for those we assist simultaneously deepens.
• Objectivity and love are not at opposite poles; in reality, they nurture one another. When we truly love in truth, we see things "as they really are." Questions of the heart lead us to this kind of love and this kind of seeing.
• Our hope as teachers and learners is to increase love for one another and for God—not to increase our love for learning. Love of learning for its own sake has no place in the education of the heart.
• Loving God's creations is akin to loving God himself. Questions of the heart can emerge from such a love and the education of the heart can increase it. Human-made objects may remind us of the love we have for others, but the education of the heart does not lead to a love of the objects themselves.

As a question growing out of freedom and love begins to take hold, we are drawn into a search for answers. The search continues as we attempt to interpret and understand the world around us, and our purposes as we live in this world.

THE
SEARCH

THE SEARCH

Questions of the heart emerge on their own; we don't sit down one day and decide to create them. They come through the natural course of living the way God wants us to live, through complete personal freedom. But once a question comes, it demands our full attention; we are compelled to action, not by force but by faith, not by external imposition but by internal submission. The search for truth, for an answer, lays hold on our whole soul, sparing nothing. We cannot rest, we cannot feel peace until we have found the answer or until the answer has found us. We must wait at times, wondering if the answer is obtainable, but then, without warning, it arrives—often in a form that we did not expect, usually in a way that teaches us more than we set out to learn.

As we search for an answer to our question, others may not notice that our approach to learning is any different than theirs. They may see us reading, studying, practicing, rehearsing, experimenting—all fairly standard approaches to learning. But the education of the heart takes place in the soul; it is not a set of techniques one goes through to master a new topic. And it is through the search itself that the soul is changed. The education of the heart causes much more than cognitive growth; it causes a change of heart.

Even major critics of education like Allan Bloom miss the point of where it all ought to lead. Nibley's (1989) response to Bloom reminds us that the education of the heart must be directed beyond this life to the eternal:

> Allan Bloom argues, "The real motive of education [is] the search for the good life." Oh, no, it isn't. See, he is limited to this world, and that makes the whole thing very sad. When we wear those caps and gowns improperly, we also receive a certificate that testifies not that we know anything, or have learned

anything, but that we have completed a course, a cursus, meaning one turn around the race track. This we think of as preparation for a *career,* which is actually the same word, *carrière* [meaning] "one complete circling of the track." In both cases it means a circular course, as the word plainly states—you are really going nowhere. Once around and that is the end. (Nibley, 1989, p. 536)

The search for truth demands a different response than does traditional learning. It demands that we have faith, that we ponder and pray, and that we open ourselves to guidance from others and from God. There must be no pretense that such a search will be easy. Exercising faith, pondering, praying, and listening for guidance require our utmost commitment, our maximum energy, our whole being. It is not a search that we can enter and exit when a bell rings in a school building, when a class starts and stops, when a semester begins and ends, or when a degree is conferred. Once we have taken our first step on the path, we must follow it to its conclusion.

How are we then to conduct such a search? What does it mean to study? What is the role of faith in seeking answers to our questions? What does it mean to ponder and pray as we learn? How can we invite and open ourselves to guidance from others and from God?

CHAPTER FOUR

STUDY AND FAITH

And as all have not faith, seek ye diligently and teach one another words of wisdom; yea, seek ye out of the best books words of wisdom; seek learning, even by study and also by faith. (Doctrine & Covenants 88:118)

In our homes and schools we have forgotten what it means to study. If I were to ask a child or a youth the meaning of the word, my respondent would likely say, "That's when you do your homework." Some might even equate it to the type of "drudgery" often attached with learning (see Chapter Two). People seldom think of great experiences when they think of the word *study*.

We have also forgotten what it means to rely on faith in our learning. *Faith* is often used narrowly to define a specific religious tradition or denomination, but it is much broader than that. Faith affects everything we do, everything we say, and everything we are. Any time we change for the better—even in seemingly insignificant ways—it is because of faith. Our belief in who we are and what we might become rests on faith. And because the education of the heart encompasses all aspects of becoming, it too rests on faith.

What, then, are the roles of study and faith in our learning? Can we rediscover the meaning of the terms and their relationship to teaching and learning? How can study and faith help us find answers to questions of the heart?

STUDY AND LEARNING

In the education of the heart, study takes on new meaning—meaning that was once tied to study but has largely been lost, at least in our current conversation about teaching and learning. Consider, for example, the difference between the word *study* used as a noun and as a verb. When we use the word as a noun, it can mean a research *study* (an experiment) or a specific room or place where one studies. It can even take on the meaning of the French word *étude,* a word that has such specific connotations that we have adopted it into English (e.g., a musical *étude).* When we think of the verb *to study,* however, we usually think of the act of reading a text and trying to understand or memorize something— with the emphasis on the *effort* we are putting forth in the process.

What do these various senses have to offer us in the education of the heart? First, our study must be centered on a question, one that springs from love and aims us toward truth. When our study is focused in this way, it becomes very different from study that is imposed on us, the kind of study we often do for tests. And even though it is self-directed, it is not self-centered; proper study is always a social act: we will inevitably want to share what we have learned. This kind of study grows out of personal interest; it is not something we must force ourselves to do. And because there is neither internal nor external force involved in proper study, it lifts us rather than weighs us down; it releases rather than drains our energy.

In the education of the heart, study connects us to others and to God. The French definition of the word *étude* approaches the meaning I am seeking: *Application méthodique de l'esprit, cherchant à comprendre et à apprendre* (Imbs, 1973, p. 305). The definition can be translated quite literally: *"the systematic application of the spirit, searching to understand and to learn."* The French dictionary follows this definition with this context phrase: *"Les deux seuls biens que je demande, l'étude et le repos"* (Constant, *Journaux,* 1804, p. 159, cited in Imbs, 1973, p. 305), which is translated: "The only two gifts that I request, study and rest."

I translated *l'esprit* as *spirit,* even though it can also be trans- lated as *mind.* An even more appropriate word would be *soul.* It is the soul that yearns to know. This is why study must involve our whole being, our spirit as well as our body. I like Constant's exam- ple because it puts emphasis on the energy we must exert when we study. As he so aptly put it, we must have both study and rest. We cannot always be exerting the kind of energy that study demands, but neither should we have too much rest, even though our culture seeks much more after rest (relaxation, leisure) than study or learning. Because television is our main form of relaxation, it has become our main replacement for study, obliterating effective education from the majority of our homes. Study deepens our knowledge of truth, expands our vision, and enriches our lives. Typical television programs do none of these; they simply entertain.

Proper study is two-way, whether we are "talking" with a study partner, with an author from the past, or with God. The conversation between reader and author is alive because our response, our sense of purpose, and our commitment to truth make it alive. Sacred text should not be viewed as ancient words written to civilizations of the past but as living words written to us as individuals (see 1 Nephi 19:23). That is why our study of sacred text can change with every reading—because our response changes each time our heart is changed, and our heart can only be changed with divine intervention. As Lévinas teaches, this kind of study turns scripture into living words that speak to us in the present ("saying") rather than dead words from the past ("have said") that have lost their meaning. Thus study forges links between us and our fellow beings, between us and our forebears, and between us and God. Their "saying" can find a place in us because even though they cannot physically manifest themselves to us, they can spiritually renew us.

Study is always a prelude to something greater—to some work that awaits our contribution. It is preparatory; it is never an end in itself. Like the question of the heart that gives rise to it, study is based upon "affection and devotion to another's welfare" (Simpson & Weiner, 1989, p. 979). That is precisely why most students and teachers misunderstand the word study—because students and teachers never get to that greater work, the welfare of another. So it becomes easy to fall into the trap of seeing study as the goal (e.g., "if you spend the next fifteen minutes studying, you can go out and play") rather than the route we follow to reach the goal ("Study and strive to acquire the knowledge that leads toward . . . the goal of life eternal," Smith, 1978, p. 206).

FORMS OF STUDY

The education of the heart embraces all forms of appropriate study—that which is directed toward truth with the ultimate aim of benefiting others. Reading, memorizing, observing, experimenting, and rehearsing—these can all be part of the education of the heart, but the way we approach these activities—these ways of searching—takes on a different nature in this kind of study.

Study and reading. In the education of the heart we read regularly, but we become much more selective in what we read. We recognize that our reading time is limited and so we spend our limited time with only the best authors. Because our reading becomes more focused on questions of the heart, we read with greater purpose and involvement. Books that are recommended by family and friends take a unique place in our reading because these are the people who know us best.

Whatever the topic, we should always keep sacred text in mind. While we need to place high value on "reading out of the best books," we must cherish the word of God in scripture. Regular scripture reading and prayer are integral to the education of the heart because they allow God to participate with us in our search. If we carry a prayerful feeling with us always, we will not limit our prayers to the times when we think we should pray, but we will be constantly drawn heavenward by the attitude of prayer that we carry in our hearts.

Our society has largely forgotten what it means to read with a real purpose, rather than simply to fulfill an assignment; to read only the best books; and to read sacred text as the word of God rather than as literature. Our youth seldom experience this kind of reading in their study, primarily because the family has abdicated its responsibility to oversee children's learning.

Study and memorization. We have also lost another aspect of appropriate study that was once integral to learning and teaching: memorization. The stereotypical image remains of the stern nineteenth-century schoolmarm demanding that a student stand and recite a poem or repeat the times tables. We can imagine her standing over the student with a ruler in her hand, poised and ready to strike the student's knuckles at the first sign of a mistake (see Travers, 1983). Recitation was seen as the centerpiece of learning and teaching. Students had not *learned* something until they could *recite it by heart.*

Current educational movements, such as "constructivism" and "critical thinking," have continued the push away from memorization and toward "higher order" thinking, reflection, and understanding. Proponents of these movements have argued, as did those in the progressive movement nearly a century ago, that memorization is too often mindless, mechanical, and pointless, and that it does not lead to deep understanding.

There is no doubt that recitation, as it was once used in schools, had serious shortcomings as a primary approach to learning. But in our haste to move away from recitation toward richer forms of learning, we have nearly abandoned it, and in the process we have lost something essential to the education of the heart. The stories and verse that were once handed down from one generation to another in family gatherings and in schools have been supplanted by television. We no longer need to remember anything written because we believe that our rendition of the story or the lines would never be as good as the one that Hollywood has produced, a version that we can rent on a moment's notice at the corner video store.

But there is an enormous difference between watching someone on a video and learning the lines, the music, or the verse ourselves. When we commit sacred text, great literature, great music, or great art or dance to memory, we store it in our heart—hence the term "learn by heart." Even this phrase originated from the ancient injunction that we should "write" the things of God on our heart. In Proverbs 3:3 we read: "Let not mercy and truth forsake thee: bind them about thy neck; *write them upon the table of thine heart."* Just as the finger of the Lord wrote the ten commandments on tables of stone, we are to write his law on our hearts (see 2 Corinthians 3:2-3); only then will we "know our place" (see Young, 1978, p. 224).

Too many of our youth do not "know their place" because they have never attached themselves to the word of God; they have never found truth and written it on their hearts. We "write something on our hearts" because we care deeply about it, because it lifts us, inspires us, and helps us to find a higher path. Only when we have written something on our heart can we "listen" to the words or the music or "see" the artistic image. Knowing the truth, and writing it on our heart, can make us free—free to experience renewal of the soul spontaneously, without having the text (or music or image) in view.

The most powerful instances of memorization occur when we discover that a phrase, a line, or a verse has been written on our heart without any conscious effort of our own. "The words are already there; we just need to find them" (personal communication, A. H. King, June 23, 1994). I believe that these instances occur when we read and reread a passage so often, believe it so strongly, and finally love it so much that we discover one day that we know the passage by heart. It is because our heart has become involved in our learning; our learning has become whole-souled. We have found truth, and it has found us because it was with us from our beginning, and it will never again be separated from us.

Study and observation. When we engage in appropriate study, we see with our hearts as well as with our minds. Parker Palmer (1993) calls it "seeing with both eyes" (p. xi). This is very different from seeing with cold objectivity, distancing ourselves from the observed so that we can remain unbiased. To the contrary, proper study requires that we observe with our whole soul—that we become involved with the observed—withholding nothing.

When we observe in this way we can respond with greater spontaneity to those around us. The botanist I described in the previous chapter who rolled up his pants and jumped into the canal reacted spontaneously because he was observing with both his spirit and his body; he was seeing "with both eyes." It was far from a thoughtless act even though he did not take time to consciously consider his alternatives. His act was unrehearsed, impromptu, because he had already "rehearsed" (engaged in appropriate study) so much that he was ready for the "performance." This is why he knew in his heart that jumping in the canal was the right thing to do.

When we observe in effective study, the world takes on a newness because our questions of the heart cause us to see and experience the world in new ways. Paraphrasing Albert Szent-Georgyi, the Nobel laureate: To search for an answer to a question of the heart "is to see what everyone else has seen and think what no one else has thought" (Regis, 1987). This does not mean that we will always be led to new scientific discoveries, new medical treatments, new symphonies, or new gymnastic movements: it means that we will come to understand things in new ways that will eventually change the way we live and help us "find our place."

Study, experimentation, and rehearsal. When we give ourselves to study we become one with the object of our study, with others, and with God. We see the object anew, just as we see ourselves anew because this kind of study always leads us to truth—which is ultimately unified in One. Study cannot be viewed as a matching exercise between topic and study method. Because truth is unified and whole, so must our study be unified and whole. Study aims higher than subject-specific pedagogy even though Shulman (1990) and others make a compelling case for treating each discipline separately. Rather than focusing on the uniqueness of topics, appropriate study focuses on the unity of topics because it aims us toward truth, which is unified and whole.

If we again consider the French word *étude,* we can understand more clearly how study can lead to similar approaches regardless of the question we are pursuing. We usually use the word *étude* in English to refer to compositions designed to help musicians improve their technique (see Randel, 1986). For example, I remember as a teenager practicing Carl Czerny's études for the keyboard. More recently the word has also come to refer to concert pieces, such as Chopin's études or "Pagannini's Caprices, which provided a fertile source of inspiration for other composers" (Arnold, 1983, p. 647). In French, however, the word refers not only to music, but to other art forms such as painting and sculpture (e.g., the sketches by the artist, Constable, of his own hands before he began to produce his final paintings; or the detailed drawings by Charles Le Brun of the paintings he later produced for the Palace of Versailles).

I am acquainted with an artist who said, while talking to a group of young people about how he found his niche as an artist:

> When I was your age I kept drawing these pictures of strange little creatures and hiding them under my bed. I never showed them to anybody because to me the pictures were just *doodling.* Frankly, I didn't think anybody else would ever want to look at them. But I kept on drawing them because it felt like that was what I was supposed to be doing. And then one day I showed my little creatures to someone, and I was shocked to find that he liked them. I started painting these little creatures and people actually started paying money for my pictures. The way I see it, I'm just getting paid now to do what I enjoyed doing when I was your age. (James Christensen, personal communication, September 23, 1993)

Although he did not recognize it in his youth, my friend was producing études that would later be the centerpieces of his work as an artist. Like musicians who practice études before performing a concerto, my friend was sketching études prior to completing his larger paintings. In either case, the artist or the musician is finding the form or developing technique—working out the detail—so that the final work in its wholeness will be "right." But artists and musicians are not the only ones who produce études. All disciplines have their preliminary attempts at finding the form and developing technique—working out the detail. Scientists complete exploratory studies before conducting extensive research projects. Authors write essays or short stories before completing a book-length work. Athletes exercise and drill before playing the game. Performers rehearse. Engineers and architects build models. Attorneys conduct mock trials.

All such attempts help learners to pay attention to detail in new ways so that they can eventually see the whole in new ways (see Zwicky, 1992). Proper study helps us to experience the "spaces between." Herman Baumann, an internationally recognized musician, once said, "The difference between a great performance and a good performance is what happens in the spaces *between the notes*" (quoted by Ralph Woodward, personal communication, March 14, 1994). It is this kind of attention to detail that makes great music great. But if performers, athletes, engineers, or scientists get bogged down in detail to the point that they lose sight of the whole, their final contribution will be second rate, will be too mechanical, or may not even emerge at all. This is why we attempt preliminary *études*—to see if we can find the balance between the detail and the whole, sense the multiplicity, and discover the unity.

But *études* in any discipline are not necessarily synonymous with study. If our motives are ill-placed, we may come to see some of the necessary details, some of the initial form, but we will never see the whole in its completeness. Only when our study is whole-souled—whole-hearted, whole-minded, and whole-bodied—will we come to see how all of the details flow together in one, how they fit together in truth. This is what study is all about in the education of the heart. Study is a form of testing, but not in the way we usually think of testing—not in multiple choice questions, percentile rankings, or scores and grades. Rather study (if we engage in it with our whole soul) is one way that we allow God to test our heart—to see if we have set our heart upon the right things (see Deuteronomy 32:46; Proverbs 15:28; and Doctrine & Covenants 121:35-36).

And if our heart is set aright—if our motives are pure—we

will come to see the unity of all that we are trying to learn. If our heart is not set aright, we will miss the unity and sink deeper into confusion. As Arthur Henry King (1986) has said:

> If we think that something is good but neither beautiful nor true, our idea of goodness is wrong. And if we think that something is true but neither beautiful nor good, then our idea of truth is wrong. If we think that something is beautiful but neither true nor good, our idea of beauty is wrong. (p. 125)

When we engage in study we will see the unity of the good, the true, and the beautiful, and our hearts will be transformed as a result. As we come to see the wholeness of all that is around us, we will be made more whole ourselves. Our heart and mind will be one.

Study and service. Proper study fits us for service, and so it is through service that we learn our most important lessons. When we serve others we integrate all that we know and all that we are able to do. Service is *the* discipline that encompasses what we consider to be "the disciplines." Because we are serving whole human beings, our approach cannot be half-hearted or half-witted; it must be whole-souled. This is the kind of service that grows out of our study—service that helps us understand how everything fits together in unity and how we can use this unity to bless others. And because service usually requires some sort of physical labor, it is through service that we see the unity of the heart, the head, and the hand. In the education of the heart "manual labor" is never considered to be less than "mental labor"; rather, it is the way we express our wholeness, our integration. In this wholeness all types of labor are revered because labor that is devoted to the benefit of another becomes a labor of the soul.

There is a stark difference between this unity of studies through service and "integrated curriculum" or "thematic units"—education's current answers to the problem of finding unity among the disciplines. While most attempts to "integrate" curriculum are pointed in the right direction, they begin with the wrong premise—that it is the teacher's responsibility to show students how the disciplines connect. In the education of the heart it is the student's question that drives the process, not the teacher. The teacher is there as a guide to help students prepare and serve, not as a dispenser of pre-packaged, integrated curricula. When a question of the heart gives rise to the student's study, the study will naturally take the student in many directions until the answer is found. These multidirectional searches will bring to light the oneness of truth without the need for lengthy explanations from a teacher about "content integration."

Aaron's project. When my third son, Aaron, was about twelve years old he needed to write his congressman to complete one of the requirements for the *Citizenship in the Nation* merit badge in scouting. After discussing possible topics for the letter, he finally settled on the issue of alcohol advertising. He wrote his congressman to request that alcohol advertising be banned from television, just like cigarette advertising had been banned decades before. The congressman never replied.

Five years later, after Aaron had been elected as vice president of his high school student body, he came to me the summer before his senior year and asked what he might do in his new role as president of the student senate. "This is the first year we've really had a student senate, and I want to do something that will be useful. But I'm not sure what kinds of things we should tackle," he said.

We talked at some length about possible issues that he might bring to the student senate, but he finally settled on the issue he had explored as a young scout: alcohol advertising. He had always been somewhat disappointed that his letter to the congressman had triggered no response. This time he wanted an answer.

Several weeks before his senior year would begin, he wrote letters of inquiry to organizations he thought might have an interest in the issue of alcohol advertising. He also visited with a professor who was a member of the state alcohol commission. The professor took an interest in my son's project and one week later came to my office to deliver a stack of materials on alcohol advertising for Aaron to read. Within another week Aaron had responses from several organizations, such as Mothers Against Drunk Driving (MADD) and Students Against Drunk Driving (SADD). One of the officers in the SADD organization telephoned Aaron to discuss his project at greater length. He suggested that Aaron contact a physician in Salt Lake City (forty miles from our home) who was a national leader in the movement to regulate alcohol advertising, the Alcohol Policy Coalition.

Aaron read the materials that were sent to him, but he was still not completely satisfied because he had not received a response from the Surgeon General's office in Washington, D.C. I told Aaron that he might never receive the response, just as he had not received one from his congressman five years earlier. But within a few days, a large package was delivered from the Surgeon General's Office containing lengthy documents on national alcohol policy, laws on drunk driving, and a recent speech given by the Surgeon General on the need to curb alcohol advertising—particularly the advertising aimed intentionally at the nation's youth.

Aaron contacted the physician in Salt Lake, began attending the coalition's monthly meetings, and was soon made an official member of their board. He learned that a bill had been submitted in Congress that would require alcohol companies to follow their televised advertisements with a message describing the health risks of alcohol consumption. The theory behind the bill was that alcohol bottlers would then eventually remove their advertisements from television rather than pay for the negative messages that would be attached to their ads.

Drawing upon advice and counsel he had received from the physician, the professor, and the national organizations, Aaron determined that he would launch a letter-writing campaign in his school aimed at getting the alcohol advertising bill passed in Congress. He spent hours drafting the original version of the one-page letter; he then copied it and asked the student senate to distribute it to all students in the school—giving students the option of signing it, discarding it, or submitting their own modified letter. After several months of work, he had collected several thousand letters—not only from his own school but from other schools in the state where students had heard about the project.

Toward the end of the school year, I had to attend a conference in Washington, D.C., so I asked Aaron if he would like to accompany me and deliver a batch of letters in person. He called the congressman from our district with the request and was given an appointment the week of my conference. Aaron found that the national director of the organization that was fighting for passage of the alcohol advertising bill was located directly across the street from our hotel. Aaron had been communicating with this man for nearly a year but had never met him. When Aaron visited with him on the first day of our stay, the man suggested that Aaron attend the meeting two days later at which the new version of the bill would be formally introduced into Congress by Senators Thurmond and Simon, and Congressman Kennedy. I attended the meeting with Aaron in a packed room of the Rayburn building. The next day Aaron visited personally with the congressman from our state and delivered three thousand letters to him. The congressman conversed with Aaron about his project, accepted the letters, and encouraged him to continue his efforts to gain passage of the bill.

Aaron learned about alcohol advertising in the course of completing his project, but he also learned about the legislative process, about good writing, about lobbyists, and about how organizations work for the public good. He read, he observed, he experimented, he memorized, he listened, and he served. His service naturally caused him to search for answers to a wide array of questions, such as What or who are the forces that are fighting against the bill? Why was it relatively easy to ban cigarette advertising from television, but so difficult to ban alcohol advertising—when it can be argued that alcohol abuse is more destructive than tobacco abuse? Who is voting against the bill and why? How have states regulated alcohol advertising? How do these state restrictions apply to the federal legislation? What laws are at issue in the regulation of the advertising of a legal substance? In fact, his questions never ended; as soon he had answered one question, a new one would take its place.

No one was pushing Aaron to continue with his project. He received a great deal of support from various mentors, but it was his decision and no one else's to pursue the project in the first place and continue on with it. After his high school year ended, he kept following the bill in Congress and kept attending the state alcohol policy coalition meetings at his own expense. His purpose was not to learn but to serve. However, as an observer throughout his project, I can attest to his learning. And I believe it is the kind of learning that will lead to other more important learning as Aaron's life continues to unfold (see *Class Notes,* #3). As Arthur Henry King (1986) has said,

> One of the mistakes we make over and over again in life is to go directly for the things we think are important. But if we aim at self-fulfillment, we shall never be fulfilled. If we aim at education, we shall never become educated. If we aim at salvation, we shall never be saved. These things are indirect, supreme results of doing something else; and the something else is *service,* it is righteousness, it is trying to do the right thing, the thing that needs to be done at each moment. (p. 255, italics added)

FAITH AND LEARNING

Our society is in the midst of a crisis of faith. I am not referring only to a reduction in religiosity; I am referring to a diminishing of all kinds of faith—faith in one another and faith in ourselves—as well as faith in God. No amount of tinkering with the edges of learning and teaching will deliver us from our present difficulties until we first examine our lack of faith.

When I was a young faculty member in New York, a colleague

in the office next to mine appeared in my doorway and, without saying anything to prepare me for his comment, announced, "You know, there's a big difference between you and me. You have faith and I don't." I was taken aback by his comment and was not certain how to respond. However, if he were to say the same thing to me today, I believe I would answer him in this way: "And what makes you think you don't have faith? I suppose you mean that I believe in God and you don't—is that it? You're saying I'm religious and you're not? But I believe you have more faith than you give yourself credit for. You may not believe in God, but you still have faith. You have faith that I will not slam the door in your face when you come to see me; you have faith that your parents will help you if you ask them for help; and you have faith that if you study hard, you will learn something. You have more faith than you think."

I like the divine appeal of Gordon B. Hinckley, now president of the LDS church:

> I say again, as did the Apostles to Jesus, "Lord, increase our faith." Grant us faith to look beyond the problems of the moment to the miracles of the future. . . .
>
> Father, grant us faith to follow counsel in the little things that can mean so very much. . . .
>
> Lord, increase our faith in one another, and in ourselves, and in our capacity to do good and great things. . . .
>
> Father, increase our faith. Of all our needs, I think the greatest is an increase in faith. And so, dear Father, increase our faith in Thee, and in Thy Beloved Son, in Thy great eternal work, in ourselves as Thy children, and in our capacity to go and do according to Thy will, and Thy precepts. (1987, p. 54)

Faith in ourselves. The education of the heart requires that we have faith in ourselves. This principle has nothing to do with self-esteem, which is a self-conscious and ultimately self-centered substitute for faith. To have faith in ourselves is to understand who we are, to know our purpose, and to trust that our purposes—our reasons for being created—can be fulfilled. Thus to have faith in ourselves is actually selfless because our purpose is to assist others. It is a faith that we can do "good and great things" for others. In the education of the heart, our study prepares us to do these good and great things: "good" because our acts are virtuous; "great," *not* because our acts attract the acclaim of the world, but because we are fulfilling the unique purposes for which we were created.

As our faith in ourselves increases, so does our ability to study effectively. We trust enough to try. We are not afraid to attack what appear to be impossible learning tasks; we are willing to apply ourselves, to "study things out" in our minds (see Doctrine & Covenants 9:88); and we come to understand that faith in ourselves is not something we seek, making it self-centered, but something that increases naturally as we exercise our faith in God. Our study then begins to take on a new flavor because once we understand our purpose, what we "need to do," we cannot be afraid to work for its accomplishment because we know that we shall have divine help.

One of the most daunting learning tasks students must face at a university is the doctoral dissertation. Identifying a question, designing the study, collecting and analyzing the data, and writing the results—these are tasks that frighten most doctoral students. And their fear often does not subside until they have successfully defended the dissertation in their final oral exam.

Several years ago some students and I conducted a series of studies with young children who were being tutored by students receiving special education services. Part of the data was used as a dissertation for an exceptionally capable student who was working with me. After months of tutoring, we began to test. When I went to pick the student up at one of the schools, I could tell there was something wrong. He had completed half of the testing, but the data were not encouraging. He said,

"What if we don't find anything worth reporting? What if all of this has been for nothing?" I looked back, wondering what I could say that would help him.

"Don't worry," I said, "the data will be all right when we finish all of the testing."

But as I drove away, I wondered why I'd been so sure. What if he was right? I thought. What if all the months of work *had* been for nothing? But the next week when we completed the testing, the data were even more positive than we had hoped in the beginning. Faith won out.

Faith in others. Just as inflation subtly whittles away at the value of the dollar, so moral decay eats away at our faith in others. We do not feel safe walking our streets at night. We cannot leave anything unlocked or unattended. We must teach our children to be suspicious of strangers. This lack of faith in others affects us more deeply than we realize. If we follow this path far enough, it leads to chronic cynicism—the belief that "human conduct is motivated wholly by self-interest" (see *Websters*, 1993, p. 289). The less faith we have in others the more selfish we become.

When others fall short we cannot allow ourselves to stop trusting them. The student completing the dissertation had to have faith in himself—faith that he could accomplish the task at hand—but he also had to have faith in others. He had to trust that teachers would assist him appropriately and that special education children would be able to follow directions. He had to have faith that the first graders could learn. He had to have faith that he could complete his study—as we all do, regardless of the form our study takes. He had already completed several pilot studies (his "études"), but he still needed increased faith to be able to complete his final project.

My son Aaron also had to have faith in other people in order to pursue his project on alcohol advertising. The physician, the professor, and the organization leaders who sent him materials and telephoned him—all these eventually drew some measure of Aaron's trust and confidence. He did not always agree with their advice, but he learned to develop confidence in them as individuals and to listen to their counsel.

When teachers and students trust one another, learning

increases. This kind of trust, or faith, must exist between student and teacher if they are to assist one another in searching for answers to questions of the heart. This does not mean that when we have faith in others we are blind to their shortcomings; we simply do not condemn them for their shortcomings. We accept their humanness and their imperfections while helping them grow through our confidence in them. It is this kind of faith that parents and children must have in each other—a faith that family members have each other's best interest at heart. It is a faith that requires all that we can give.

Faith in God. All faith eventually finds its way to God. Some, like my office partner in New York, may never acknowledge it, but it is God nonetheless who is "the author and finisher of our faith" (see Hebrews 12:2). To have faith in ourselves or in one another is to have faith in God because he is our creator, the father of our spirit. To have faith in his offspring is ultimately to have faith in him. And until we recognize this, our learning will always be limited because our aim will always be too low.

It is the voice of God within us, whether we recognize it or not, that causes us to look outside ourselves to search for truth. We sense that there is something more, something higher, some connection between the ground we stand on and the heavens that surround us. As our faith increases and we engage in proper study, we will find the mysteries of God opening to our view. An ancient prophet, King Benjamin, once said: "I have not commanded you to come up hither to trifle with the words which I shall speak, but that you should hearken unto me, and open your ears that ye may hear, and your hearts that ye may understand, and your minds that the mysteries of God may be unfolded to your view" (Mosiah 2:9).

Only when we open our hearts will God's mysteries open to us. We may become expert in a given discipline, in the knowledge or riches of the world, but we will never learn of eternal things until we open our hearts and have faith in him. In the education of the heart, we search for increased faith while we search for an answer to our question. It is in the seeking for and deepening of our faith that our answer will come. This is because our dual search gradually becomes one search, a search for truth, a search for God: "Seek not for riches but for wisdom, and behold, the mysteries of God shall be unfolded unto you, and then shall you be made rich. Behold, he that hath eternal life is rich" (Doctrine & Covenants 6:7).

The education of the heart leads to "spiritual and intellectual unity" (see Benson, in Welch, 1988). When we learn in faith, we see the oneness of all that surrounds us and feel a oneness with our creator. Brigham Young said, "All who keep the faith are of one heart and one mind, and this testimony is so confirmed to all that we cannot be mistaken" (Young, 1978, p. 282, 18:231).

As we learn in faith, our faith in our own ability to attack new learning tasks and our faith in others naturally increase. But if our faith never goes beyond the "arm of the flesh," we will never experience the education of the heart.

As portrayed in the movie *Lorenzo's Oil,* the Odones had to have a certain amount of faith in their own ability to tackle a difficult scientific problem, one that the medical community had not yet solved; but they also had to have faith in others and eventually in God. At times their faith was shaken because others did not respond in ways that the Odones believed they should. But the fact remains that the Odones could not have found a cure for their son's disease without the help of others.

The movie script makes no outward mention of faith in divine help. But I found it interesting that the music, which was prominently featured in the movie, had a religious theme. The only negative review of the movie I was able to find criticized the selection of music for its religious overtones. The reviewer thought that such music made the movie too heavy, too serious. Until reading this review, I had not paid close attention to the music. But as I listened more carefully to the music, I came to disagree with the reviewer and side with those who had produced the movie. I believe the music was intended to show that the Odones' search was based not only on faith in themselves and faith in each other, but faith in God. Their search drew them closer to God, as all searches of the heart do.

When we exercise our faith in God as learners and teachers, we find that his arm is always extended. Our faith in him is the most intensely personal aspect of our life. He will enlighten us if we will only allow him in. His power to assist us in our learning is infinite. He will lead us to truth if we open ourselves and submit our whole souls in faith to him. We will learn of eternal things because our hearts will be cleansed and ready to receive his living water: "Let us draw near with a true heart in full assurance of faith, having our hearts sprinkled from an evil conscience, and our bodies washed with pure water" (Hebrews 10:22).

Watchwords
• Study ties us to others and to God. It is a process of affection because our study has the ultimate aim of benefiting others. Proper study grows out of love.
• Study allows us to see the details we have never seen before, but it also allows us to see how the details fit together to form a whole.
• When we engage in study we aim toward truth. This requires that we search with our whole being, withholding nothing.
• Study can take many forms, but the forms appear on the surface to vary more than they do in reality. All disciplines demand some sort of initial attempts *(études)* that are preliminary to achieving some greater goal and teach us about the overall shape and fit of what we are studying.
• Memorization should have a place in our study—not mindless, mechanical memorization, but the "writing of the Word on our heart."
• We must have faith in ourselves, in others, and in God if we are to find answers to our questions of the heart.
• Having faith in the "arm of flesh" is not enough. Our faith as learners and teachers must eventually be grounded and rooted in God.
• When we exercise faith as learners and teachers, we will discover the mysteries of God that will lead us to life eternal.

When one searches for an answer by study and faith, one is naturally led to ponder and pray. These are inevitable steps for a faithful seeker of truth.

CHAPTER FIVE

PONDERING AND PRAYER

But Mary kept all these things, and
pondered [them] in her heart. (Luke 2:19)

When Christ visited his "other sheep" on this continent, as recounted in the Book of Mormon, he could see that they were having difficulty understanding what he was teaching them, so he asked them to return to their homes to ponder and pray about what he had taught (see 3 Nephi 17:2-3). He did not try a second time to teach them the principles he knew they did not yet understand; rather, he asked them to return to their homes where they could reflect on his message, discuss it with those who were closest to them, and then pray for deeper understanding.

As we face our own learning challenges, eventually we are led to ponder and pray. To ponder is to weigh, to contemplate, to compare—to try thoughts on to see how they fit. Just as Christ wanted the Nephites to do more than "think" about his message, so too we must include pondering in our own serious study. Pondering cannot be rushed; it must occur on its own time and in its own way. It is an individual activity that takes on different characteristics for every soul. Pondering often leads to prayer because as we exert ourselves spiritually to solve a problem we are naturally drawn to God. How should the act of pondering affect our learning and teaching? What is the role of prayer? What is the role of each in the learning and teaching that take place in the education of the heart?

PONDERING

The process of pondering begins as we open ourselves to a question, as we consider alternative ways of looking at a problem, as we allow thought to find a place in us—a place that eventually involves us completely. When we contemplate, meditate, or reflect, we approach the process of pondering, but pondering goes further. Pondering is more focused, more sustained; rather than leading us only to new insights or intuitions, it leads us to sound judgment and conviction.

Pondering requires a specific problem, a question to be answered, some sort of perplexity. Only when we struggle with uncertainty are we drawn to ponder over a solution. J. T. Dillon (1988) has said:

> The main event at the start of [learning] is the experience of perplexity. That is the precondition of questioning and thus the prerequisite for learning. Questioning still might not follow, nor learning; without perplexity [questioning or learning] cannot follow. (p. 18)

Perplexities that occupy us in the education of the heart focus on the needs of others—other students, other teachers, our children, our parents, or our friends. Pondering is thus a private activity that may eventually lead to a public good.

Pondering and truth. Rather than focusing on the self, the ultimate aim of pondering is finding truth. This is why our study must include pondering over the question we are trying to answer. The type of question is immaterial; we might be puzzled about a musical composition, a poem we are trying to write, a scientific study we are conducting, or a math problem we are trying to solve. Andrew Wiles, a Princeton mathematician, is a good example of one who was captured by a question, one that mathematicians had been unable to solve for 350 years—Fermat's last theorem. He began trying to solve the theorem in his youth, as had many other budding mathematicians, but he kept working on the solution during his formal education and then during his career as a professor—never letting the question go. As Kolata tells the story—

[Fermat's] theorem is deceptively simple to state. It says that there are no positive whole numbers that solve the equation $x^n + y^n = z^n$ when n is greater than 2. When n is 2, solutions are easy to find. For example, $3^2 + 4^2 = 5^2$. But that, by Fermat's last theorem, is the end of the line. There are no solutions when n is 3 or any greater number.

The son of a theologian at Oxford University in England, Andrew Wiles first came across Fermat's last theorem when he was ten years old and saw it in a book in his town's public library. He has forgotten the book's title and author, but he vividly remembers its effect. It made him want to be a mathematician, and it made him want to solve the problem. "I spent much of my teenage years trying to prove it," Dr. Wiles recalled. "It was always in the back of my mind."

Then two professors at distant universities suggested to Wiles that if a mathematical proposition they were working on could be proved true, Fermat's theorem would also be proved true. Because the proposition they were working on was so essential to other mathematical issues, these two professors made Fermat's theorem something the rest of the mathematics world could not ignore. So Wiles continued to work on the solution at home in "a barren attic office" with no interruptions.

Dr. Wiles worked feverishly on it. "Basically, I restricted myself to my work and my family," Dr. Wiles said. "I don't think I ever stopped working on it. It was on my mind all the time. Once you're really desperate to find the answer to something, you can't let go," he said.

Then, while reading a paper by a Harvard mathematician, Wiles saw that by using the "construction" he had read about in the paper, he could complete the solution to his problem.

The construction, as it happened, was not new. It dates to the nineteenth century. But Dr. Wiles had not heard of it before. As soon as he saw it, Dr. Wiles said, "I knew I had it." He could complete his seven-year quest and proof of Fermat's last theorem

(Kolata, 1993, pp. 8-10).

Andrew Wiles was seeking a solution. As with anyone who is captured by a question, he could not let it go until he had found an answer. And it was through pondering that the solution came. Some might conclude that Wiles' question was not a question of the heart because it seemed strictly intellectual and not aimed at helping anyone else. I will not attempt to judge his motives in solving Fermat's theorem, but I found it particularly interesting that after he had solved the problem, he felt a certain kind of sadness along with his exhilaration.

"All number theorists, deep down, feel that," he said. "For many of us, [Fermat's] problem drew us in and we always considered it something you dream about but never actually do." Now, he said, "There is a sense of loss, actually" (p. 10).

Wiles' sense of loss came from losing something that had become a part of him. The question was no longer there because he had solved it—even though other questions undoubtedly grew out of his proposed solution. And he had not solved it only for himself; he had solved it for *all* number theorists who, like himself, had also been captured by the problem. Once he had perfected the proof, he no longer had the same relationship with his colleagues, and none of them could ever again have the same relationship to the problem that bound them together. However, new problems certainly would emerge that would lead to new relationships and new solutions. Wiles was searching for a truth, and he put his whole being into it. In my view, he was engaged in the education of the heart.

Pondering and place. Andrew Wiles went to his attic office to ponder the solution to Fermat's theorem. This was his place of study—likely a place where he could be alone for a certain period of time. Our culture no longer attaches much importance to place. We uproot ourselves at a moment's notice when our employer calls with a "transfer." We buy televisions for nearly every room in the house and put cellular telephones in our cars so that wherever we are we will have "access." When the agrarian age ended, so did the importance of place, and now that we have entered an era of "technopoly," as Neil Postman (1992) calls it, we continue to move further away from the connection our forebears had with the place they called home.

I grew up on a plot of land that was once the farm of my mother's parents. When my great-grandfather began farming there in the late 1800s, his fellow farmers were convinced that he would never be able to turn a profit. Because the farm was located at the foot of the Rocky Mountains, his friends believed that the growing season would be too short for crops to mature. But my great-grandfather persisted and became a successful fruit farmer, as did my grandfather after him. When my grandfather died, he gave a plot of land to each of his children. My parents built a home on their plot when I was a young boy.

Now when my mother looks out her window, she sees other homes, yards, and black-top streets. Sometimes when she sits back and ponders the experiences she had in her childhood and youth, she sees the old farm where she grew up—a rich, fertile place where row after row of dewberries pestered her each season with their prickly thorns and where apple, peach, and pear trees yielded bushels of fruit each year.

Just before my nineteen-year-old son was to leave home for a Church mission in Italy, my mother took him on a tour of the old farm. She wanted to help him see what she sees when she looks out upon the place of her birth. She showed him the old apple tree where grandpa used to catch a few minutes of intermittent sleep when he was irrigating his fruit trees at night. She showed him the old home where she was born and grew to adulthood. She walked with him to the creek that ran through her yard where she remembers fetching water for drinking and washing. And finally, she stood with him under the pear tree where her father was found after his heart had stopped beating—a tree that had grown from a seedling that his son had given to him "so that dad could have a pear orchard."

My mother wanted my son to take with him something of the

place that meant so much to her. Although she may not have used these exact words, she wanted my son to understand how our learning can give meaning to a place, and how a place can then give rise to our learning. She wanted him to understand that physical location affects our ability to ponder, and that when pondering occurs in the right place, it can lead us to singular truths about our own identity and about our inseparable ties to one another. As Wendell Berry has said: "As never before I'm impressed with the dependence of a human place, such as a farm, on human love" (p. 43).

We all need places where we can ponder, places where we can see what no one else can see. In these places we can find a firmness of hope in the midst of the complexities and perplexities that sometimes engulf us. We can sense the importance of our own purpose; we can, through study, find truth.

Pondering and purity of heart. When the angel Gabriel counseled Mary to ponder in her heart the things she had heard and seen, he knew that Mary's heart was pure. And because her heart was pure, Gabriel knew that she would come to understand the message he had delivered, a message that would potentially change the lives of all who would ponder, pray, and believe.

Effective study demands that our motives be pure. If we are to find truth through pondering and prayer, we must set our hearts not upon the things of the world, but upon the things of God. God's ways are simple, clear, and unpretentious. The world's ways are complex, blurry, and self-aggrandizing. Only when our hearts are right can we ponder the things that will lead us to truth. James E. Talmage (1976) recounts the story of Nicodemus coming to Christ, asking what was necessary for salvation. Christ responded to a ruler of Israel by saying—

> "Verily, verily, I say unto thee, Except a man be born of water and of the Spirit, he cannot enter into the kingdom of God. That which is born of the flesh is flesh; and that which is born of the Spirit is spirit. Marvel not that I said unto thee, Ye must be born again." Still the learned Jew *pondered* yet failed to

comprehend. Possibly the sound of the night breeze was heard at that moment; if so, Jesus was but utilizing the incident as a skillful teacher when He continued: "The wind bloweth where it listeth, and thou hearest the sound thereof, but canst not tell whence it cometh, and whither it goeth: so is every one that is born of the Spirit." (pp. 160-161, italics added)

Nicodemus pondered what Christ had said, but his heart was not pure in the process; he was still thinking of the world, its knowledge, and its power. Thus his pondering did not help him "comprehend" truth; he could hear the "wind" but did not recognize its source; he could see Jesus but did not know who he really was. For this reason, when our heart is clouded with the things of the world, we can have "eyes . . . but see not" and "ears . . . but hear not" (Psalms 115:5-6). Only when our heart is pure can our pondering lead us to truth.

Pondering and individuals. In the education of the heart, parents and teachers have a particular responsibility to ponder over their children and students. We must ponder their needs as individuals and consider how we, who have been charged with their care might help them fulfill those needs. Pondering helps us discern and understand the unique nature of each student or child. By pondering over those we teach, we come to understand their true potential as human beings and our role in helping them reach that potential. We can learn to look beyond outward appearance and see individuals as they might become. Our goal is to take the counsel the Lord gave to Samuel when he was selecting a son of Jesse to be anointed king. When Samuel saw Eliab, the prophet believed that surely he would be the one. However, Samuel was told to look further:

> But the Lord said unto Samuel, Look not on his countenance, or on the height of his stature; because I have refused him: for [the Lord seeth] not as man seeth; for man looketh on the outward appearance, but the Lord looketh on the heart. (1 Samuel 16:7)

Samuel met each of Jesse's sons but was still not satisfied that he had identified the right one. He asked if Jesse had other sons and found that there was one more who "keepeth the sheep." Samuel asked that David be brought before him. When he saw David, he apparently looked upon his heart and knew at once that he should be anointed king. He saw David's potential even though he was young and inexperienced, just as we must see the potential of those we teach.

Pondering over our students helps us as teachers to examine ourselves as teachers (see *Class Notes, #4*). We come to understand how we must adapt our teaching if we are to benefit those we serve. If we focus on the individual, not on ourselves, we can change to meet the needs of those we teach. In today's educational system, such adaptation might be viewed by some as a luxury, something we cannot afford to pay teachers to do. A teacher's job, after all, is to teach, not to think about teaching. But such an approach leads to mindless education; it leads to doing things for the wrong reasons because we forget what our reasons are. We lose sight of truth.

> Getting the job done is good. Pondering how the job should be done, or whether or not it should be done, is apt to be regarded as a waste of time. If we want coal, it seems to us perfectly feasible to destroy a mountain or a valley in order to get it. (Berry, 1989, p. 106)

Berry is cautioning us against mistreating our environment. We are already coming to view this kind of mistreatment as mindless. But what about the mistreatment of our children? I am not referring only to the horrors we read daily in the news-papers about child abuse. I mean the more subtle kinds of mis-treatment that occur every day in homes and schools because as parents and teachers we focus on the outwardly visible, tangible needs of children, but forget the intangible inner needs of the individual. These are the needs we must ponder if we are to help the next generation fulfill its promise.

Pondering and moral decisions. In the education of the heart, teaching and learning are both moral acts—teaching because it is one person attempting to help another, learning because it must be based upon what we can do for others. As teachers and parents we must constantly ask ourselves, "What is the right (moral, ethical) thing to do?" As Lévinas (1993a) so clearly points out, every time we respond to another human being, we are acting on some sort of ethic. Pondering the question "What is the right thing to do?" we come to find truth or allow it to find us. I like Victor Frankl's account in his current preface to *Man's Search for Meaning* in which he explains why he did not try to escape from Austria after Hitler and his troops had occupied the country. He had received an invitation from the American Consulate to come to Vienna and retrieve his visa for the U.S. Upon arriving in Vienna, his aging parents rejoiced with him that he would soon be able to leave the occupied country and emigrate to America.

But then he was faced with a question: Could he in good conscience leave his parents alone in Austria to meet their inevitable fate in a concentration or extermination camp? What should he do—follow his parents' wishes and leave the country where he could write his books and continue building his profession, or should he stay and try to protect his parents? Where did his responsibility lie? He *pondered* the problem but he could not solve it. He began wishing for "a hint from Heaven."

> "It was then that I noticed a piece of marble lying on a table at home. When I asked my father about it, he explained that he had found it on the site where the National Socialists had burned down the largest Viennese synagogue. He had taken the piece home because it was part of the tables on which the Ten Commandments were inscribed. One gilded Hebrew letter was engraved on the piece; my father explained that this letter stood for one of the Commandments. Eagerly I asked, 'Which one is it?' He answered, 'Honor thy father and thy mother that thy

days may be long upon the land.' At that moment I decided to stay with my father and my mother upon the land, and to let the American visa lapse" (Frankl, 1992, p. 13, italics added).

I believe that Frankl's *pondering* helped him see the significance of the engravings on the marble slab. Had he not thought deeply and pondered his decision in his heart, he likely would not have recognized the message as a "hint from heaven." His eyes were ready to see because his heart was right, and his heart was right because he had pondered.

PRAYER

In addition to pondering, we must strive to carry with us an attitude of prayer; only then will our minds and hearts be prepared to see truth. After recounting the parable of the lord in the vineyard, Christ admonished his listeners to ponder the message and determine its meaning for them personally: "And again, verily I say unto you, my friends, I leave these sayings with you to ponder in your hearts, with this commandment which I give unto you, that ye shall call upon me while I am near" (Doctrine & Covenants 88:62).

Christ did not ask his listeners to complete any written assignments; he did not ask them to prepare for a written test on the meaning of the parable. He asked them simply to ponder and then to call upon him. He knew that if they would do these two things, "the eyes of [their] understanding would be opened" (Doctrine & Covenants 138:11). He also knew that if they did not follow his counsel, their hearts would not be prepared to see with new understanding; even though they might have heard his parable, they would not be able to act upon it in their own lives. Through pondering and prayer, we prepare ourselves to learn. This is why they are such essential parts of study, regardless of the question we are pursuing.

Prayer and the heart. Our hearts should be lifted up in prayer continually (see Doctrine & Covenants 30:6). Prayer is not limited to the words we utter when we make a formal appeal to God; prayer is an attitude of heart, something we carry with us always. We are to "pray without ceasing" (1 Thessalonians 5:17, Mosiah 26:39). This is why pondering and prayer go together. When we are searching for an answer—considering the direction we should go—our hearts are naturally drawn to pray. Not until we pray, not until we are in an attitude or condition of prayer, can we be certain that we are following the path that God would have us follow.

> But behold, I say unto you that ye must pray always, and not faint; that ye must not perform any thing unto the Lord save in the first place ye shall pray unto the Father in the name of Christ, that he will consecrate thy performance unto thee, that thy performance may be for the welfare of thy soul. (2 Nephi 32:9)

Our prayers need not be perfectly worded. When we are seeking an answer to a question of the heart, we need only have a heart that is set aright:

> In praying, though a person's words be few and awkwardly expressed, if the heart is pure before God, that prayer will avail more than the eloquence of a Cicero. What does the Lord, the Father of us all, care about our mode of expression? The simple, honest heart is of more avail with the Lord than all the pomp, pride, splendor, and eloquence produced by men. When he looks upon a heart full of sincerity, integrity, and child-like simplicity, he sees a principle that will endure forever—That is the spirit . . . the spirit I have given to my children. (Young, 1978, p. 169)

Prayer and faith. Along with whatever we are learning, we should always be praying for an increase of faith, as did the apostles of old: "And the apostles said unto the Lord, Increase our faith" (Luke 17:5). During our search for answers, our faith will always increase at the same time our knowledge increases. As we pray in faith, nothing wavering, we come to see things as they really are, and when our eyes open to this view, our faith in God naturally increases.

Prayer and power. Power as defined by politicians is inherently different than power as defined by God. Political power is measured in terms of control and domination; God's power is measured in dimensions of benevolence, discernment, and edification. Control and domination are artificial creations of those who seek power in the worldly definition; benevolence, discernment, and edification are qualities of the heart. As teachers and learners, we should pray for God's power to be in us, to lift us, and to make us capable of doing the things that we are meant to do. We should likewise pray that we might avoid the illusion of the worldly impostors of power that surround us constantly, who find their way into classrooms as often as they find their ways into boardrooms or bedrooms.

As an undergraduate student I enrolled in a statistics course to fill one of the requirements for my major. One day a young woman sitting next to me raised her hand and timidly asked a question about a principle the teacher had just finished explaining. As soon as she had uttered the words, I sensed that the teacher would not take kindly to her question. He was one who knew he was in control and relished it. He looked at my friend, and with an unmistakable harshness in his voice said, "I just got through explaining that. What happened? Were you daydreaming about your date last night? I don't answer questions when people don't listen." There were approximately ten students in the class, and I believe that all ten felt the pain that my friend was feeling. She never asked another question in class.

While this teacher was wielding a sort of power, it was not the kind of power that comes from God. When we follow God's ways through study and prayer, we receive a completely different kind of power, including the power to teach, whether we are teaching as parents, as friends, or as teachers in a classroom: "But this is not all; they had given themselves to much prayer, and fasting; therefore they had the spirit of prophecy, and the spirit of revelation, and when they taught, they taught with power and authority of God" (Alma 17:3).

The power and authority of God allow us to see as God sees, to hear as God hears, and to know as God knows. This power allows us to respond to others with love rather than in anger or insensitivity. God's power allows us to respond as Christ did to the woman who had committed adultery: "Neither do I condemn thee: go, and sin no more" (John 8:11).

"Then spake Jesus again unto them, saying, I am the light of the world: he that followeth me shall not walk in darkness, but shall have the light of life" (John 8:12).

The Pharisees never escaped the darkness they were in, and they never saw the light that Christ brought because their eyes were clouded over with the images and ideas of the world. Thus they were continually confused by Jesus' stories. Jesus' disciples were enlightened because they felt his power; the Pharisees were merely disdainful because they believed that their knowledge was superior to his.

How different Christ's power is from the concept of "empowerment" that is finding its way into most schools, businesses, and even homes. Schools that are "empowered" have "site-based" management programs, teachers who have the right to select their own curriculum, and students who have the right to choose more of what they want to learn. Employees are empowered in businesses to make their own decisions. Children are empowered in homes to live how they want to live rather than how their parents want them to live.

But these concepts of power are all based upon artificial control and domination. They depend to some extent on mistrust among partners: the child mistrusts the parent, the employee mistrusts the supervisor, the school principal mistrusts the district superintendent—leading to an eventual mistrust of the organization of which they are a part. Our mistrust often ends up focused on an institution rather than on a real person. So we conclude that we need to be empowered to stand up to these nameless entities.

Jesus, however, always used his power to forgive in love. His only motive was to help others. Knowing the hearts of others, he acted out of trust rather than skepticism, love rather than arrogance. And he enjoined us to do the same, to be even as he is. This is why we should pray for the power to learn how we can discern the needs of others and be of greater service to those around us.

Prayer and learning. When we are young we learn to pray so that when we are older we can pray to learn. We pray for wisdom, knowledge, and understanding. We pray for answers to our questions of the heart: to know what and how we should study, and how and from whom we should seek guidance. We live in a day of unprecedented availability of information. Not only has more been written and recorded in the present era than in any other period of the world's history, but the information is also easier to retrieve because of the electronic age. What once took weeks to search out now takes minutes. With electronic databases, catalogues, and media resources, our search takes on a different nature than it might have just ten years ago.

The proliferation of resources has made our search more potentially rewarding but at the same time more potentially challenging. We cannot seek information from *all* sources; we must be discriminating. And this is where prayer comes in. We need to pray for guidance in our search, for the kind of guidance that will help us find answers to the questions that capture us. Invariably, this guidance will include other people who know more about our question than we do and are willing to help us on our way. Through such people, God answers our prayers and helps us answer the questions of the heart.

Watchwords

• Pondering involves considering, contemplating, meditating, weighing, and valuing. When we ponder, we try new thoughts on to see how they fit—to see if they help us solve a problem. Pondering is the way out of thoughtlessness.

• Unless we ponder, we will never obtain an answer to our questions of the heart. These questions demand pondering because they reside deep within us.

• While studying can take a variety of forms, pondering is an activity of the soul. It requires unity of spirit and body, heart and mind. Only when we feel unity will we find our answer.

• Pondering is not limited to a single discipline. As an ingredient in study, it helps us see more deeply into a topic but also helps us understand how our topic connects to other topics and to truth.

• While many forms of study are social, pondering is largely private. It can be sparked by human or divine intervention, but it finally must occur within us. Pondering is what takes place in the "spaces" between our encounters with others.

• Pondering can be effective only when our heart is pure. Our purity of heart is a matter between God and us, not between others and ourselves.

• We can deepen our pondering when we recognize the importance of place in nurturing the pondering heart. A place that draws us closer to our roots and reminds us who we are can also draw us closer to truth and hence nearer to God.

• Prayer acknowledges our own nothingness and recognizes the power of God to rectify our nothingness.

• As we pray for answers to our questions of the heart, we also pray for an increase of faith.

• Through prayer we can feel the power of the Almighty, a power that differs completely from worldly power.

• In the education of the heart, we must pray without ceasing. Our heart should always be drawn up unto prayer. Just as pondering takes place in the "spaces"—life's quiet intermissions—so does prayer.

• Our prayers focus on our questions of the heart. Through prayer we learn to see, hear, and know as God does because prayer connects us to God and to all his creations.

CHAPTER SIX

GUIDANCE

I will instruct thee and teach thee in the way which thou shalt go: I will guide thee with mine eye. (Psalm 32:8)

When my oldest son, Russell, was twelve years old, his scoutmaster announced that the troop would be going spelunking. Having never explored a cave, my son was excited, particularly when he heard that the cave went "straight down in the ground, like a hole going to the center of the earth." After they had hiked to the cave's opening, the scoutmaster asked, "Who wants to be the first one to go down into the cave?" My son volunteered and soon began lowering himself down the narrow walls of the cave, holding tightly to a rope which the scoutmaster had provided. As Russell descended, the cave became increasingly dark until he could see nothing. He got his flashlight out of his pocket so he could see where he was going but dropped it as he kept hold of the rope.

When he came to the end of the rope, the scoutmaster yelled to him, "Have you reached the bottom?" My son yelled back, "There's no more rope, but I can't feel the bottom yet!" The scoutmaster responded, "Just let go, you're almost there." Russell let go of the rope and dropped only a foot or two onto the floor of the cave.

My son's experience is similar to one that I had as an assistant scoutmaster. However, rather than lowering ourselves into a cave, our troop was backpacking up a mountain to a meadow where we planned to camp overnight. Some scouts were able to hike much faster than others, so I volunteered to stay back with those who were progressing more slowly, making certain that we did not leave anyone behind. The boy furthest back on the trail was small for his age and was carrying a backpack that appeared to weigh almost as much as he did. I convinced him to leave his six-pack of soda pop on the trail to be retrieved the next day on our way down the mountain. This made his pack lighter, but not light enough.

We finally reached a meadow and the boy said, "Is this the meadow we're going to camp in tonight?" Pointing about twenty feet away, I said, "No, our meadow is just across that stream and over that ridge." Without saying anything he removed his back-pack and sat down on the ground. "Do you want to rest for a minute?" I asked. "No, I'm going to sleep here tonight," he said firmly, "I'm not going one more step." I explained to him that even though we could not see the next meadow because of the ridge, it was only a few feet away from where he was now sitting. Unconvinced, he did not move. I sat down next to him; we rested, talked some more, and then he suddenly stood up, put the pack on his back, and began walking toward the ridge. We finally fin-ished the last twenty feet of the hike.

In both instances the scoutmaster and I were acting as guides for the scouts. A guide is one who "leads or shows the way." To be an effective guide one must possess two attributes: (1) knowledge of the terrain, and (2) knowledge of the traveler. If the guide knows nothing of the terrain, both the guide and the traveler will likely go astray. But if the guide knows only the terrain and noth-ing about the traveler's interests and abilities, the entire expedition could be in vain. In my son's case the scoutmaster knew the length of the rope and depth of the cave; he knew that my son would not drop far if he let go of the rope. In the straggler's case, I knew our destination, but I also knew the boy, and I wanted to see him make it on his own without my having to carry his pack for him.

In the education of the heart, we seek guidance as we search for answers to our questions, guidance from those who know something of the topic we are pursuing, and who also come to know us. Because our guide accompanies us on our journey, we develop a trust in one another that always comes when we are seeking truth. Our guide is not there to dispense truth but to show us the way to find it—knowing all the while that because truth is intimate, we shall each come to know it in our own way.

Guidance can be effective only if it is *good* guidance and if we open ourselves to it. In the education of the heart we take care to avoid guidance that would lead us away from truth, but when we have found guidance worth listening to, we listen. We recognize that most of what passes for guidance in the modern world—information dissemination—merits little of our attention. Rather than filling our minds with empty messages of the mass media, we seek to fill our hearts with truths that resonate inside us, and which as they resonate grow ever deeper and richer. Thus we prepare ourselves to receive truth at the same moment that we seek the guidance that will lead us to it. We can never relax in either direction: we must be constantly vigilant in seeking only the best guidance, and we must also keep our hearts ready for the guidance we receive. This is the only way to seek truth and allow it to seek us.

When guidance leads us to new knowledge and new understanding, we are obligated to act on it, to change the way we respond to those around us and use this new understanding to lift others. Listening to a good guide is not enough; we must actually follow where the guide leads us. When light and truth enter our hearts, we cannot rest until we have given the light and truth to someone else. This is the responsibility of one who receives guidance.

But before we can follow guidance, we must know where to find it and how to receive it.

READYING OUR HEARTS

In current educational usage, *readiness* refers to the preparation of a child to enter school or to learn to read. The concept of readiness has never been well defined, but we accept it as a necessary prerequisite for good education. Educators and parents seem to agree that one cannot teach a child before the child is *ready* to learn. But what does it mean to be ready to learn? We can all recognize a child who enters school who is not ready, but how do we know when the child *is* ready? A student recently recounted to me how she developed an aversion to math. She said, "It all happened when I was in the eighth grade. I got stuck in pre-algebra and never could get back out. I guess I just wasn't ready for what they were teaching—I don't know— but I *do* know that I have had a fear of math ever since."

This student's experience shows that readiness applies not only to young children, but to older learners as well. In fact, readiness affects our learning throughout our lives. I am not referring to the common meaning of readiness—cognitive or physical development—but to the readiness of the heart. This kind of readiness determines whether we are prepared to receive truth. It is a desire for wisdom, a yearning for virtue. It has little to with cognitive development and much to do with the development of the whole person.

Examples of *unready* hearts are prevalent. As a twenty-year-old LDS missionary in Tahiti, I remember meeting a Frenchman who invited us into his home. We soon discovered, however, that he had no intention of listening to our message; rather, he wanted to convince us that he was more educated than we were—that his vocabulary was greater than ours, and that he understood the things of the "cosmos," as he put it, better than we did. We resisted the temptation to argue with him and finally left on good terms, but it was clear to us that his heart was not ready to receive our message; he was too caught up in his own learning to learn anything new from someone else.

I also think of the time I tried to visit a young man in the youth detention center. When I asked the attendant if I could see him, she told me that she would return with him in a few minutes. But when she returned, he was not with her. "He said that he'd rather not see you right now," she told me. He did not feel comfortable facing me; his heart was not yet ready.

I have known other bright, talented youth who have lost their way. They often stopped seeking good guidance long before they were "caught." And as they stopped seeking good guidance, their hearts became hardened to the point that they were no longer comfortable in the presence of those who genuinely wanted to help them. As they became uncomfortable with those who loved them, they increasingly blocked truth's ability to enter their heart. Truth is always ready to find us, but we must be ready to let it in.

Each of the preceding chapters has offered suggestions for readying the heart to receive good guidance. A ready heart is one that has a question already inside. Why would one seek guidance if one had no question? This would be like calling a travel agent on the phone and then remaining silent. Only when a question of the heart is present can guidance become meaningful. Likewise a ready heart is one that is free from a desire to do evil and can therefore recognize truth when truth "knocks." A heart that is full of love and faith—a heart that studies, ponders, and prays—possesses the ingredients of real readiness. When the heart has achieved this readiness, one is prepared to receive guidance and embrace truth.

Just as the education of the heart can take place only when we are in community (see Palmer, 1993), so our hearts can be ready to learn only if we open ourselves to others and to God. The scriptures teach that part of the responsibility for a ready heart is ours: "Therefore, prepare thy heart to receive and obey the instructions which I am about to give unto you" (Doctrine & Covenants 132:3). However, the process is not complete until divine assistance comes:

> O Lord . . . keep this for ever in the imagination of the thoughts of the heart of thy people, and prepare their heart unto thee. (1 Chronicles 29:18)

> Lord, thou hast heard the desire of the humble: thou wilt prepare their heart, thou wilt cause thine ear to hear. (Psalm 10:17)

SEEKING GUIDANCE

Parker Palmer (1992) has said that "giving advice can be an act of violence." I believe he is talking about unsought advice, the kind of advice that manipulates others to the benefit of the advice giver. Advice to invest in "get-rich-quick" schemes is a prime example. The courts in Utah are currently sorting through suits concerning a multinational corporation that deceived hundreds of well-intentioned investors.

But bad advice can be given for more than financial investments. I am reminded of the advice a friend received just after she had lost her hearing, following a bout with spinal meningitis: "You should take a plane ride. I've heard that if you go up in a plane, you know, in the pressurized cabin, your hearing will come back," she was told. My friend, an accomplished pianist, chuckled as she recounted how several people had come to her with similar kinds of advice on how to get her hearing back so she could continue with her musical career, but she admitted that at the time the advice was given, it added to her pain rather than alleviating it.

How can we be sure that we are seeking the best guidance, that the advice we receive will not in some way violate our sensibilities? A ready heart is a prerequisite, but we must do more, we must seek with "real intent" to find truth. We can determine if the guidance is good by the degree to which it leads us to truth.

The guidance we seek can take many forms. It can come from books, family and friends, teachers and mentors, and God. The authors of the past can tutor us from a distance, even though they have never met us face to face. In one sense, as we come to know them, as we let their words find a place in us, these authors live on in us. Although they have never met us, we sometimes feel as if they were writing directly to us. This is particularly true of the scriptures. God reveals his will in a unique way to each of us, even though we are all reading the same words on the same pages. This is the power of the written word to teach, instruct, and lift the soul. It is the kind of guidance we seek every day.

We must not become discouraged when the guidance we seek does not come as quickly or as clearly as we would like. The Odones faced multiple obstacles as they searched for a cure for Lorenzo's disease. The medical community was at first suspicious of their efforts, the scientific community was not interested in their problem, and the Food and Drug Administration made it difficult for them to experiment with a new medication. But the Odones persisted. They did not allow outsiders, who did not fully understand their problem, to dissuade them. When they confronted someone who refused to help them, they simply sought another source. And so, eventually, the librarian, the research scientists, and the British biochemist all played significant roles in the Odones' search. At the outset the Odones could not have predicted who would help them in their search for a cure, but the guidance came as others invested themselves in the Odones' question, providing unique kinds of support that each was prepared to offer at a particular time.

Andrew Wiles apparently received guidance less directly than did the Odones. He was helped along the way by other mathematicians who were also searching for a solution to Fermat's Theorem. But, according to Wiles, his most important guidance came during a lecture by a Harvard mathematician who was not even addressing Fermat's Theorem. He gave insights that Wiles could never have predicted; he provided information that was not new in the field of mathematics, but new to Wiles. And Wiles knew as soon as he saw the "construction" that it was the missing link in his solution. He had not become discouraged by years of searching; he knew he would find a solution one day; and when it presented itself, he was ready to receive it.

Wiles' experience, however, does not mean that Harvard professors have a corner on giving guidance or that Princeton professors have a corner on receiving it. Worldly position and acclaim have nothing to do with guidance. Parents give guidance to children, teachers give guidance to students, and co-workers give guidance to each other—not because of a formal educational degree they have received, but because of a commitment they have to the other person. Ignoring the guidance of those who are less formally educated may cause us to miss the guidance that could be the most valuable.

My ethnobotanist friend conducts some of his research in the rain forests of Samoa, searching for botanical medicines unfamiliar to American physicians. He spends significant amounts of time talking with native herbal doctors—not those who have graduated from medical school and received a degree, but those who have mastered the medical uses of hundreds of plants. My friend has learned some of his most important lessons from these native Samoans and counsels his students to develop this same kind of respect as they work together with these island doctors: "I tell my students, 'If you can sit in a hut and respect the person, they can feel that no matter what. Live your life with indigenous people as if at any moment they could read your heart—because they probably can'" (quoted by McEntee, 1994, p. B3).

My father-in-law had to quit attending school in the eighth grade because his overalls had "too many holes," and he could not afford to replace them. But his lack of formal degrees did not stop him from learning. He learned to run a business, to garden, and to occupy positions of leadership in his church—all through life's experience. Even after retirement, he kept on learning. He invented a bread-mixer attachment, manufactured hundreds of them in his garage, and sold them nationally. He also developed a phonetic guide for pronouncing the foreign names of one's ancestors. I have learned from him what it means to solve problems— more than I ever could have learned by completing a course on problem-solving.

Parental guidance. A French kindergarten teacher once told me that her most difficult challenges were not with the children in her class but with their parents, who, in the teacher's opinion, were often unwilling or unable to provide their child with proper guidance. She said, "When I explained to a mother that her child was constantly kicking other children on the playground, the mother replied, 'Oh, he's always kicking me around the house, too. That's just the way he is.'" What the mother failed to realize was that by allowing her son to inflict pain on others, she was teaching him that such behavior was completely acceptable. The mother did not understand her role as a guide.

Guidance that goes from one generation to another is the cord that binds a culture, a people together. Parent-to-child guidance is a uniquely powerful form of such learning and teaching. Like teachers, parents can become confused about the meaning of freedom and learning. The mother of the French kindergarten child may have thought it was her goal to let her child run free, make his own decisions, see his mistakes, and eventually change his ways. Another parent may leap to the other extreme, restricting the child to the point that the child cannot function without the parent present. In both cases the parents have an incomplete view of personal freedom, as explained in Chapter Two. They have failed to see that every choice is a moral choice and that their own lives as parents affect their children more deeply than the verbal lessons they give when they are "parenting."

My great-grandfather lived until I was almost four years old. I can remember him sitting out on the porch in front of an old shed we called "the shanty." The shanty was full of mystery for me and for my cousins who lived next door. We knew we were not supposed to play inside it, but we never knew why. Only when Great-Grandpa was sitting on the porch, supervising us, were we allowed to enter (although we did not obey the rule all the time). We would go inside wondering if we would find a ghost or a trap door, but instead of ghosts we found fascinating objects—many of which we could not name. There were tools for making furrows in the garden, supplies for my uncle's beekeeping enterprise, equipment for shearing my uncle's sheep, and stirrups for horses we no longer had. The objects were not very orderly; some seemed not to have been used for years. When we could not name an object, we would bring it out of the shanty and ask Great-Grandpa, who would not only would tell us its name but would give us its history.

Although I learned the names of those objects when I was four years old, I doubt that I could name some of them now—or that many of my generation could name them. They were objects of another era, another way of life. Rather than being attached to animals or the soil, most of our present-day objects are attached to an electrical cord. We can differentiate "ink-jet," "laser," and "dot-matrix" printers, but we cannot draw a picture of an egg-candling device or explain its function. Being able to name objects is less important than understanding who our forebears were, how they lived their lives, and how we can learn from their example.

I remember my grandmother caring for my great-grandfather as he became bedridden during the last months of his life. I do not believe he ever went to a hospital in those final months; he died in his home surrounded by his children, his grandchildren, and his great-grandchildren. Thirty-nine years later, the cycle was repeated as my parents cared for my grandmother in her final months. These examples of caring for parents are part of the legacy of lessons that my forebears have left to me. They may have tried to teach me to be unselfish when I was younger, but I cannot remember any of these "talks"; what I do remember is their unselfishness, their willingness to place their own needs second to the needs of those they loved.

The kind of guidance that I received from my great-grandfather, my grandmother, and my parents has been slipping away from society since industrialization, and the slippage is continually picking up speed. The disintegration of the family has not only caused many children to stop caring for their parents, but it has caused many parents to abdicate their responsibility to guide their children. Many children rely more on teachers to rear them than they do on their own parents. Ernest Boyer (1994) tells how his daughter, an elementary school teacher in Boston, has students come to her every day to ask if they can stay after school rather than returning to empty, unsafe homes. As Boyer laments, "We are a society that no longer cares for its children" (1993).

In an interview with the French novelist Louis Pauwels, a

journalist commented, "So the thing that has changed most in our society is that there are no more fathers, hence the title of your book, *Les Orphelins* [Orphans]." Pauwels responded,

> In fact, this is likely one of the signs of our time. The mechanisms of transmission from one generation to the other appear to have broken down. The fact that adolescents in 1968 wanted to separate from their fathers, insisting with a desperate pride on becoming orphans—this is the evidence. But you notice that [the central character in the book] Antoine, also ignored his father. Everyone tries to make it through life with as much good as bad; but alone. This is one of the characteristics of our time. (In Suffert, 1994, p. 32)

There is no need to rehearse statistics; we are all well acquainted with those who are trying to make it through life alone—children without fathers, wives without husbands, families without each other. The more we have sought self-fulfillment, self-actualization, self-awareness, and self-esteem, the more we have distanced ourselves from the ones who can teach us who we really are. We have failed to recognize that as our ties to our earthly parents have unraveled, so have our ties to our heavenly parents. And as these ties have weakened, so has our ability to receive guidance weakened. Guidance from family members and guidance from God are correlated much as the soundtrack and video are synchronized in a movie: when you turn one off, you have a hard time benefiting from the other.

Guidance from God. There was a time when God was the focus of western culture: visual arts, music, literature, architecture—the creations of human hands—reflected the hand of our creator. But the concert halls of today are seldom filled with new religious music; our museums of contemporary art are not dominated by religious paintings; and our bookstore shelves are not filled with religious books. The Enlightenment, in spite of the "progress" that it has brought, has gradually moved us further away from our real source of light. As we have objectified our world, we have not only moved further away from the earth by exploiting her resources, but have lost sight of heaven as well. And with the de-glorification of God, we have had nothing left to glorify but the "self," a philosophical invention of modernism. The university naturally replaced the temple—not as the giver of truth, because truth became indefinable, but as the giver of knowledge. And as knowledge has replaced truth, we no longer sense a need for God as our guide because we can create "facts" and master them on our own.

Those who do not believe in eternity see no need for a guide that is eternal: if one's most important destination is a career, a career counselor will suffice. But for those who have reached their life's goal—whatever it may be—and feel emptiness instead of peace and wholeness, guidance from God becomes their only hope. Questions of the heart spring from such hope, a hope that leads us away from the transitory world to a realization of our eternal nature. We are drawn to God because our question demands heavenly intervention.

God's guidance can come in many forms, most of them subtle and simple, all of them personal. When Joseph Smith read the passage in James, the words were more than prophetic writing; they were God speaking directly to Joseph himself. This is the kind of guidance that is available to all of us who will simply read God's word. But God sends messengers as well as messages. Some of his messengers are anointed servants; others are friends or family members. Ruth of the Old Testament would not leave her widowed mother-in-law, Naomi, who felt "empty" upon her return to Bethlehem after the death of her husband and both of her sons. But guidance came from God to both of them—through both of them to each other—as the emptiness was filled with the birth of a son they called Obed, through whose lineage came the one who is the "root and the offspring of David, the bright and morning star."

Ruth's story reminds us that in following God's guidance we

must do what virtue compels us to do. Orpah, the other daughter-in-law, returned to her home and to her Moabite God, but Ruth could not. Not only did Ruth love Naomi, but she had come to know and love Naomi's God. She could not leave her mother-in-law alone with no one to care for her. Naomi likely knew that Ruth would remain with her, even though Naomi told her repeatedly to go back to her people. And once together, they gave guidance and support to each other: Rather than seeking self-fulfillment, they sought the fulfillment of prophecy and of their purposes in the Lord.

The story of Ruth and Naomi does not mean that God's guidance can come only through family members. I am acquainted with a professor who has devoted his life to providing guidance in a way that makes God's purposes transparent. He does not teach subjects; he teaches individuals, not out of duty or by authority, but out of love and by the Spirit of God. He is completely honest and naturally humorous. Having no children of his own, he "adopts" some students, much as Ruth and Naomi adopted one another. As I have experienced his guidance myself, I have wondered why more teaching is not so inspired and why more learning is not like my learning when I am with him. I have concluded that the answer comes back to a question of seeking. As long as one seeks learning for learning's sake, one cannot be genuinely learned, and as long as one seeks good teaching for teaching's sake, one cannot be a good teacher. Life's demands, life's questions must be the driving force behind being a good guide, as well as an effective receiver of guidance.

ACTING ON GUIDANCE

Readying our hearts, seeking for answers, and listening to guidance are not enough; we have not *learned* until we have acted on the guidance we have received. If we are learning to play a musical instrument, we must practice often. If we are learning a new defensive move in basketball, we must try to execute it. This is when guidance can become the most essential, when we are experimenting with a new skill or with a new way of acting or thinking. This is when the one with more experience, the one who has traveled the path before us, can help us refine an idea, polish a talent, or smooth the rough edges on an incomplete skill.

The guide must at this point be sensitive to the limits of the learner, yet at the same time be impeccably honest. A teacher does not help by complimenting poor performance, but if the teacher expects more than a student is capable of producing on a given day, there is a risk of aborting the learning task permanently. When I was about ten years old, I enrolled in a swimming class. Because I was tall for my age the teacher seemed to think that I would be able to skip the basics and move up to the next level. On the first day of instruction, the teacher marched us all down to the end of the pool with the diving boards and asked us to dive in and swim the length of the pool. I had never been in water over my head, let alone tried to dive and swim a pool length. When I told the teacher that I thought it would be a good idea if I learned to swim first, he just said, "Oh, you're a big kid. You can do it."

I give the man credit for seeing that I was taller than others in my age group, but I don't count him as a good teacher. I was stubborn enough that I would not dive in the deep end; I finally walked back into the locker room and never came back for another lesson. The teacher was teaching swimming as a topic; he was not teaching me as a person. I eventually came to enjoy swimming but not because of this particular teacher. As a teacher myself, I have come to understand better the difficulties this teacher faced. Knowing each student and responding to each student appropriately is a challenge of the highest order.

I once had a student with a severe hearing impairment come to me and tell me that she wanted to study at Juilliard School of Music and become an opera star. She asked me to listen to her voice and tell her what I thought. I played a few notes on the piano and asked her to sing each note as I played it. Her voice quality was satisfactory, but she had a problem which was understandable, given the severity of her hearing impairment: she could not match pitch. She often came close to matching a note, but never sang exactly on pitch. I struggled with the kind of guidance I should give to her. Stories ran through my mind about how teachers had turned students away from something they wanted to pursue—stories like my own experience with the swimming teacher. But I had to be honest. I told her that she had difficulty matching pitch and that learning to sing would continue to be a challenge with the type of hearing impairment she had. She was not angry or upset but seemed almost grateful to receive honest feedback.

My wife teaches beginning piano to students of all ages. I have noticed that her guidance changes with each student and varies with the same student on different days. She is completely honest. When a student needs correction, she corrects. But her corrections are always given in a way that encourages rather than demoralizes the student. "You can do it," she says, "but you need to count right here and then it will be perfect." She knows when to ease off and when to have the student repeat a section "just one more time." She gives guidance that is at the same time honest and encouraging. She helps one student be less compulsive and another be a little more exacting.

The student who has trouble with the rhythm in a certain section goes home and practices that section repeatedly (we hope). The student who needs to become less mechanical and more expressive goes home and practices the piece with expression in mind. I do not offer these illustrations as methods that others could use to improve their teaching, but as examples of how we must act on the guidance we receive. It is never enough to read a good book, listen to a teacher, or pray for wisdom; we must change the way we approach life.

When we act on the guidance we receive, we find that not only are we led closer to truth but we also deepen the relationship with the guide. We discover that family relationships are not static, but always changing; we are either growing closer together or further apart—and one of the most important factors affecting our relationships with other family members is how we give and receive guidance. With limited familiarity with the French language, Lisa, my fourteen-year-old daughter, enrolled in a Parisian "Collège" (junior high school). Deciphering the notes to parents, purchasing the right kinds of paper and writing instruments, and determining what time her classes would begin the next day were major hurdles. But somehow she survived, and I am convinced that her survival is a direct result of others in the family who rallied around her, giving her the support and guidance she needed at each juncture. As Pauwels (1994) has said, *"Survivre est souvant une affaire de relations"* ("Survival often depends on relationships") (p. 12).

In the story of the prodigal son, we naturally focus on the scene of the wayward one returning home: "But when [the son] was yet a great way off, his father saw him, and had compassion, and ran, and fell on his neck, and kissed him" (Luke 15:20). We seldom consider the kind of parental guidance that led to the son's return. He had been taught as a child to keep the commandments of God but chose to take his inheritance and waste it on "riotous living." Then, while he was carrying out his daily task of "feeding the swine," he began to ponder his own behavior. He remembered, I believe, the teachings of his father and knew that he needed to reconcile himself with the one whose confidence he had betrayed.

The son rehearsed privately the words he would say to his father because he knew the words would be difficult to utter when he actually saw his father face to face: "Father, I have sinned against heaven, and in thy sight, and am no more worthy to be called thy son." It was during these moments of rehearsal that the son's heart was changed, that he became so humble that he was willing to be his father's "hired servant" rather than his son. These were moments of personal reconciliation, when he made peace with himself. Then he went to make peace with his father, the one whom he had offended. When the son returned home, I am convinced that he knew his father would forgive him and accept him again into the family; the years of guidance he had received from his father told him so. He knew his father and his father knew him. And once he had made peace with his earthly father, he became reconciled with his Father in Heaven. The son's willingness to change his way of living, to obey the truth that was inside him, naturally drew him closer to his family and to God. Repentance always strengthens eternal relationships.

Experimenting on the word. When prophets receive guidance, they follow it; when they convey that same guidance to us, we often ignore it. We make the mistake of thinking that prophets are speaking about religious topics that do not concern everyday life, rather than seeing that everyday life is at its base a religious experience. Moses did what the Lord told him to do—he led the children of Israel to the promised land, but the people themselves were slow to understand, so slow that they were required to spend forty years in the wilderness so that the Lord could "know what [was] in [their] heart, whether [they would] keep his commandments, or no" (Deuteronomy 8:2). The God seems harsh who would force a people to spend forty years in the wilderness proving themselves.

I once had a colleague in developmental psychology at another institution ask me why the God of the Old Testament was so different from the God of the New Testament. I responded, "Perhaps, because he knew his children and had to teach them differently." He liked the response because it fit his own ideas about human development. God gives guidance that his children can understand, and if his children have wholly turned to idolatry, the guidance will be different than if they are wholly committed to loving the Lord and their neighbor. In effect, the Israelites experimented on the word of God until they became convinced that his way was the truth and that idols were false gods. Like all societal changes, the change that came over the Israelites took more than one generation to accomplish.

When we receive guidance that we believe will lead us to truth, we must "experiment" on the word. We must "plant the seed, nourish it, and let it sprout, to see if it is a good seed" (Alma

32:27, 33). We must follow the word of God until we see the effects in our own lives and the lives of those around us. If the guidance is leading us toward truth, we will recognize its power in our lives to lift us, bolster our faith, and increase our love for others. If the guidance does not lead us to truth, we will feel a loss of power and a decrease of faith and love for others. This is precisely how one generation cleaves to the good and discards the bad that has come to them from their forebears. We must act on guidance, question the assumptions of our current generation, and change the way we live. In this way our search for answers to questions of the heart will yield fruits that nourish us for eternity.

Watchwords

• Guidance can take root in us only when our heart is ready. Readiness comes as we are captured by a question, as we study, exercise our faith, ponder, and pray.

• As we ready ourselves to receive guidance we open our heart to truth. Having an open heart means that we become susceptible to the prompting and tutoring of honest guides.

• Guidance leads us away from confusion into clarity, from thirst to running water that is freely given.

• The ability to give and receive guidance does not come from diplomas, certificates, or licenses; we can learn more from the humble who think they know nothing at all than we can from the haughty who think they know everything.

• Although we actively seek guidance, we recognize that guidance is also actively seeking us, and that it often comes in unexpected ways, reminding us that learning is seldom merely linear and that teaching, if done properly, is seldom predictable or systematic.

• Effective guides lead us to truth, to the place we know we must go to fulfill our purpose for being, but they may take us there by a route and by means that differ sharply from the ones we would have chosen on our own.

• While even the most effective guidance may not lead us immediately to a satisfying resolution, we are constantly reminded that being on the right path is more important than reaching our final destination. We realize that some final destinations require a life-long search.

• When we act on guidance we "experiment on the word": we let it find a place in us, allow it to change the ways we see the world and respond to others, and rely on it to help us learn.

• Guidance is an intentional act to assist others, but the guide's intent is to invite rather than compel, to offer rather than constrain. The intent of the one who questions is what matters most. The guide acts in the best interest of the questioner because the questioner's interests are the guide's reason for being.

• When we recognize God as our supreme guide—the way, the truth, and the life—our ability to receive guidance and benefit from it increases, whether the guidance comes directly from God or indirectly through another person.

• Guidance connects us to others and to God, reminding us that we are tied—not only genealogically but pedagogically—to those who came before and to those who will come after. Guidance in its most primal form is parental, not in the controlling, authoritarian sense of the term, but in the loving, nurturing sense.

THE
FRUITS

THE FRUITS

When we teach, we want results (see *Class Notes,* #5). As parents we may want to see our child's behavior change; as workshop leaders we may want participants to demonstrate their mastery of a new idea that we have just presented. In each case we are looking for tangible evidence that our teaching has had the desired effect.

When we learn, we also want results. We want to know that we are making progress. Finding an answer to a question is a measurable result of our search. The medical community may reject Lorenzo's Oil as an effective cure for ALD. The mathematics community may reject Wiles' proof. Far more important than the answer to the question is what happens along the way, the changes that occur in the learner that go beyond the ability to explain a mathematical proof or isolate the ingredients in a medicine. These changes affect us as souls; they are indirect, unplanned, and unexpected. They resonate inside us through our whole being. They are at once sacred and personal. We cannot replicate them at will. They are the fruits of the education of the heart.

Naming some of the fruits might lessen them in some way because neither the list nor the description of each term could ever be complete or adequate. They are the qualities attached to the deepest, most important kind of learning that occurs, a kind of learning that our present culture has forgotten. But one reason we have lost sight of the education of the heart may be because we seldom recognize or discuss the fruits of this kind of learning and teaching. By not allowing these terms to enter into our conversations, we have come to value them less. And because we value them less, we do not experience them as often as we might.

I have selected terms to identify fruits that I believe are central to the education of the heart. These fruits should be viewed as examples only, not as a complete list. They are *sensibility, reverence, humility, edification, inspiration,* and *joy.* These are qualities that are disappearing not only from our educational system, but from our homes and individual lives. They are human qualities that tie us to God and to others. But as each of the terms has been replaced in current educational jargon with more "acceptable" substitute terms, the cords that bind us together are being weakened to the point that our relationships with each other and with God are coming unraveled. The substitute terms may appear to be innocuous or even laudatory on the surface, but I am convinced that these terms eat away at our understanding until we no longer recognize the inevitable loss of meaning in our conversations and, more importantly, in our lives.

Decision-making skills may help us list the advantages and disadvantages of a series of alternatives, but they will likely not help us increase our power of *discernment.* Focusing on *self-awareness* may actually divert us from developing *sensibility.* Trying to improve our *self-esteem* likewise may make it more difficult for us to develop humility. *Assertiveness training* may reduce our *reverence* for each other. *Cooperative learning* may lead to better relationships in the classroom, but it may not lead to *edification.* As explained in Chapter Three, *love of learning* may actually preclude us from experiencing the *joy* that comes from proper study, pondering, and prayer.

Unlike the results of traditional learning and teaching, the fruits of the education of the heart are qualities needed to pursue the education, as well as the harvest, that one experiences while conducting the search. Without *reverence* or *humility* a question of the heart cannot emerge. Without *sensibility* the learner cannot determine the adequacy or sincerity of guidance that is given. Without *inspiration* we cannot be certain that we have found truth. But as the question is posed and the search begins, each of these qualities can be enhanced if the learner's heart is open. The fruits mature as the search continues, never as the aim of the search, but as the gifts that come as conditions of engaging in the process.

The fruits of the education of the heart come to the learner, as well as to those who *know* the learner. But I will address each term from the standpoint of the one asking the question, keeping in mind that the learner never seeks the fruits directly but experiences them as indirect gifts that are freely given. Rather than saying, "Today I will be more humble," the learner says, "Today I will seek an answer to my question." And although there is nothing wrong with assessing the accuracy of our answer or the adequacy of our search, there is something wrong with measuring the fruits of the search. Because the fruits are gifts from God, we could only diminish them and ourselves by trying to measure them. We readily recognize and appreciate the fruits in others, but we do not look for them in ourselves; when they appear, however, we sense their presence because we "taste" them.

TASTE

An advertisement on French television shows a group of cheese experts tasting a new brand of cheese. Each expert in sequence shows his approval of the new cheese. When the last expert tastes the cheese, he says, "Les Américains ne l'aimeront pas." ("Americans won't like it.") In response to his comment the others spontaneously break into applause. People of different cultures take pride in their taste because taste is one way that we define ourselves.

There are few universally liked foods; water may be the only substance that we could give to people anywhere in the world and expect that they would enjoy it. In the education of the heart the universal substance is truth. Like water, all humans seek it, but unlike water, not all experience the taste of truth regularly. The process involved in the education of the heart helps seekers taste truth more often and develop a desire to seek it with their whole soul. This is at the very core of the education of the heart—to develop a desire to seek truth after experiencing the taste, a desire that ties us together as sisters and brothers, and can lead us to eternal life (see 1 Nephi 8, 11). We want to learn to avoid bitter fruits, which are poisonous and can lead to our destruction.

The more we taste the good fruit of the education of the heart, the more we want to eat it. We can never attain too much truth and light; we know that we will never gain enough in this life (Nibley, 1989). But as we constantly seek after truth, we will be filled. We will taste of the fruits that are reserved for those who seek with their whole heart and will one day say with the Psalmist: "How sweet are thy words unto my taste! [Yea, sweeter] than honey to my mouth!" (Psalm 119:103).

CHAPTER SEVEN

SENSIBILITY

Whatever hinders upward progression deadens the sensibilities and real enjoyments of this world's life. (Joseph Fielding Smith, 1978 p. 353)

On a Saturday morning in 1977 I was working inside the house when the doorbell rang. Expecting to greet a friend of one of our children, I went to the door without much haste. When I opened the door I saw my five-year-old son, Richard, standing on the threshold with blood running down his face and neck. He had been unable to enter the house on his own because the door was locked. I first thought that he had severed an artery and was bleeding to death, but as I gathered my senses and examined him more closely, I found an inch-long cut in the scalp on the back of his head and traced the source of blood to this one wound. I quickly grabbed a damp cloth, wiped the dried blood off of his face and neck, lifted him into the car, and sped to the emergency room, where a doctor had agreed to meet us. The doctor, a plastic surgeon, spent approximately forty-five minutes cleaning the wound, which was packed with debris—mostly small dirt particles and pebbles that had lodged under Richard's scalp when he had fallen as his bike struck a rock on a steep hill behind our home.

The doctor allowed me to observe the entire treatment. What caught my attention was the doctor's hands as he cleaned the debris from under Richard's scalp. He would move his thumb over the top of the scalp, feel a protrusion, lift up the skin and remove the particle of dirt or small pebble. He would then wash the wound and again use his thumb to feel for any remaining debris. I cannot recall how many times he repeated this procedure, but I do remember that he looked up at one point and said, "I want to check just one more time to see if I may have missed something. The important thing is to make sure we don't have anything left under the skin." After making one more pass with his thumb, he again looked at me and said, "We've got it." He then stitched the torn scalp together.

When I returned home to tell my wife, who had been at a friend's home on the other side of town, I told her that we had paid the doctor not so much for his ability to stitch up cuts, but for the sense of touch he had developed in his thumb. I explained how the stitching had taken a relatively short time compared to the process of cleaning the debris out of the wound, and how grateful I had been for the doctor's ability to detect the debris with a thumb that had been "well trained." Although I did not use the term at the time, I was telling my wife that I was grateful for the doctor's *sensibility*.

If I were to search through a stack of current books on education—textbooks for teacher preparation, social studies texts for junior high school students, history or English texts for high school students—I doubt that I would find the word *sensibility* in any of them. And yet it is one of the most important fruits of a good education. The term does not refer just to one's ability to "perceive through the senses," as the plastic surgeon used his sense of touch to clean my son's wound; it also includes one's ability to feel sympathy for another human being, become aware of others' needs, and react to those needs with dispatch and sincerity—a kind of *refined sensitivity*. The word also embraces the power to "make sense" of our world, the ability to perceive things clearly without confusion.

We recognize the loss of sensibilities when the loss is extreme but often fail to recognize a slight decrease that occurs slowly and subtly. When a serial killer explains that he felt no remorse for his heinous acts—or that he felt a sort of pleasure in committing them—we concur that the person has become "numb" and "past feeling," and has lost his sensibilities. But when we hear sarcasm between family members (modeled daily in our homes and on television sitcoms) or observe high school students cheating on their tests—a virtual epidemic in our nation's classrooms (see Chilcoat & Ligon, 1993)—we excuse the behavior as part of "growing up." And as we excuse such behavior, we condone it and increase its presence in our homes, neighborhoods, schools, and society. This is how whole cultures gradually lose their sensibilities.

The aim of the education of the heart is to heighten our sensibilities and increase our capacity to taste the fruits so that we can distinguish the bitter from the sweet, just as the physician learned to differentiate a clean wound from one that contained impurities. Our sensibilities are developed in the recurring activities of life, the ones we sometimes view as nonessential or even intrusive. Our search for answers is not so single-minded that we block out the rest of life while we search. We recognize that what happens in the simple, relaxed moments may be more important to our search than what happens during our most focused study. Nowhere is this more apparent than in our everyday conversation. As James counsels us in the New Testament, we should engage in "good conversation" and avoid "envying and strife in our hearts" because with envying and strife come "confusion and every evil work" (James 3:13-18).

James continues to explain the ingredients of "good conversation": it is filled with "wisdom from above that is first pure, then peaceable, gentle, and easy to be entreated, full of mercy and good fruits, without partiality, and without hypocrisy" (James 3:17). We know when we have had such conversation because we feel the better for it after it has occurred. Such conversation heightens our sensibilities; it increases our awareness of others' needs and reminds us of our own purposes in life. But we recognize that such conversation is not planned in advance. There are no scripts to be prepared and distributed to participants. Conversation simply unfolds; we do not know where it will go next. We react to the others' presence and talk, and the others respond to ours, weaving meaning into the exchange as well as into our lives. The French have much to teach Americans about such conversation: most importantly, that the conversation can occur only if we set aside time for it.

On a recent visit to France I was escorted on a tour of several educational institutions by a distinguished emeritus professor at the University of Paris. After we had visited an educational research facility, he asked if I would like to see the *Ecole Normale Supérieure*. I told him that I would enjoy seeing the school, but that I would be happy to see it on my own since he had already spent so much time with me that day. He insisted that he personally introduce me to the school. As we approached the gate a guard allowed us to enter through a back walkway because the school was closed for spring vacation. The building itself was square, surrounding an open courtyard with a traditional fountain in the center.

The professor invited me to sit with him on a bench just in front of the fountain. The wind was blowing so the water from the fountain would throw a gentle spray our way from time to time. I could sense immediately that the school meant more to him than the research institution we had visited previously. The *Ecole Normale Supérieure* was not just another French educational establishment, it was *his* school. He described how he had been one of 30 applicants out of 1000 to be admitted when he was finishing his studies at the *Lycée* over fifty years earlier, but that as soon as he began at the school, he was called up to serve in the French Résistance during World War II. Rather than spending his first year at the school, he spent it as an undercover soldier in the Swiss Alps trying to repel the Germans. He further explained that this was the school of many of the modern political leaders of France and that Sartre had taught there before gaining recognition as the promulgator of existentialism.

In the space of half an hour this man had shared something of French military history and educational history, as well as something of himself with me. When we come to know someone else more fully we come to a deeper understanding of our own reason for being. Earlier that same day, sensing my need to master French educational terms, this professor had begun keeping a list of terms with definitions in French so that I could better understand the lecture sessions we were attending. Any time we went through a door, he motioned for me to pass first. He noticed that I did not have a warm enough coat, so he brought one of his coats to me and insisted that I use it for the week I would be in Paris. One morning when we went for our *petit déjeuner* (breakfast) at the local bakery shop, he complimented the woman at the cash register on the quality of her croissant rolls. These were spontaneous acts on his part; they were his natural responses to those around him. During the week I spent with him, I learned much about the French educational system, but I learned even more about what it means to be educated.

Rather than emphasizing one sense over another, the education of the heart unifies our sensibilities so that we experience wholeness instead of fragmentation, clarity instead of confusion. We experience life through the unity of our senses as we recognize our place in the world and our place in eternity. As outside meets inside, as beginning meets end, as soul meets soul, the differences we once thought important disappear, and the differences that we overlooked become paramount. Not only can we distinguish more readily between good and evil, but we can see anew what we have seen before, hear anew what we have heard before, and know again what we have known before. We are constantly reminded that, although we may be temporary residents on earth, we really had no beginning and will have no end (see Doctrine & Covenants 93:29; also Abraham 3:18). And as our sense of place is made clearer, our ability to sense others' needs is heightened.

CHARITY

When my son appeared in the doorway covered with blood, and when the doctor told the Odones that their son had ALD disease, the parental response was immediate and spontaneous— both were acts of parental love. This love that ties families together can bind all of us if we develop charity, the most important of all sensibilities. Charity, the scriptures tell us, "is the pure love of Christ" and if we are "found possessed of it in the last day it shall be well with [us]" (Moroni 7:47). Charity is self-forgetful; it causes us to act in the other's best interest, even if the act causes us pain or death. For example, after fitting other passengers with life jackets and assisting several into the rescue apparatus, a man disappeared in the waters of the icy Potomac River following an airline disaster in Washington, D.C. His heart was set on the needs of others more than on his own well-being.

Because our search for answers to questions of the heart ultimately benefits others, the search itself might be viewed as an act of charity—even though we seldom know who the benefactors of our search will be. We know, however, that we must pursue the search if we are to fulfill our purpose, and we know that our purpose goes beyond our own needs. Our love for others increases as we continue in our study—particularly toward those who give themselves to assist us in our search. We realize that the only way to repay the ones who keep "fitting us with life jackets" is to assist others in their search for answers to life's questions. In this way the education of the heart is as much a social act as it is a deeply personal one. Such an education does not occur in isolation. We may be able to learn something while reading a book or listening to a tape, but if we keep our eyes in the book—or our ears beneath the headphones—as we walk down the sidewalk, we shall be unable to react to those who approach us. Our newfound fact will not *live* until it changes the way we respond to the others in our life. It cannot grow inside of us until we have made it transparent by allowing others to sense it. A friend once told me that his father used to say, "Love is not something you feel; it is something you *do.*"

DISCERNMENT

When our sensibilities are intact, when we are full of charity, we are able to see with the soul and hear with the heart. Not only can we distinguish between good and evil, and right and wrong, but we can know in what direction we should move—how we should live our lives. This is the power of discernment, the ability to see the difference between two things without using our eyes, to hear the difference without using our ears. Discernment involves the ability to choose one thing over another; it is a fruit that grows when we understand the role of freedom in learning; it is one of the fruits of a search that is based upon faith, a search that heightens our ability to benefit from guidance.

My wife recently enrolled in a series of music courses that emphasized "ear training." She and the other students were required to look at a sheet of music and "sight sing" the notes; they were also required to listen to note patterns played by the instructor and write the notes on their blank sheet. To pass the course, students had to demonstrate their ability to record the soprano, alto, tenor, and bass parts when played simultaneously by the teacher. The task was at first daunting. My wife would practice for hours each day, listening to tapes, writing the notes on her paper, and comparing her rendition with the answers in the workbook. Even for an experienced musician, the task was not an easy one. It required well-developed auditory discrimination.

As my wife continued with the series of courses, month after month, I noticed a marked improvement as I helped her with her nightly assignments. Picking out the bass-line in a dictation became less challenging than it had been only a few months earlier. Her ability to focus on rhythm and pitch at the same time had also clearly improved. Like my wife's experience with music, we can improve our ability to discern by consciously listening for cues that can help us remain on the path we were meant to follow. However, rather than a semester-long or year-long project, refining our power of discernment continues for a lifetime. In life, as with music dictation, it is often hard to distinguish a single part while all the other parts are being played at the same time. If we spend our time listening to the discord of "detractors," we risk losing our ability to hear the "melody" from the voice that is still and small. Knowing how to focus our attention is half the battle.

Benjamin Bloom (1974) once conducted a study that showed that the "fastest" children in a classroom were not much faster at learning than the "slowest" children when researchers measured only the time that children were actually "on task"—when the children were focusing their attention on what they were trying to learn. The slower children were slower because they generally did not focus their attention on the learning task. So it is with discernment—our ability to make correct choices increases as we focus our attention on the task at hand and rely on God to aid us in our decisions. Like the child who is distracted, we can dull our sense of discernment by listening to the clang and banter of a world that has lost its way.

Attenuation in hearing is the process of blocking out background noise so that we can hear the "signal"—something that we are constantly experiencing but seldom recognize. I once had a young adult friend with a severe hearing impairment who preferred to use sign language rather than oral communication and so had never used a hearing aid. When my colleague, an audiologist, convinced him to try a hearing aid just once, I invited them over to my home to "conduct the experiment." When the hearing aid was inserted in my friend's ear and turned on, he grimaced and said, "What's that rattly sound outside?"

I responded, "You mean the car tires making noise on the wet freeway?"

"It's so loud," he said.

Then, when the refrigerator came on, he again asked, "What's that?"

At first, I was uncertain what sound he was referring to because I had not heard the refrigerator turn on—it was a sound that I naturally attenuated. When I determined that he had heard the refrigerator, I took him over to it and showed him what was making the sound. These were sounds he had never heard before, sounds that people with normal hearing seldom hear themselves because they attenuate them.

When we allow the background noises in life to take precedence over the "signal," our power of discernment is weakened. We begin to focus on the wrong things, losing sight of our ultimate goal. The intents of our heart become clouded, and we lose direction. When we allow ourselves to be drawn to the background noises and indulge in them, we dull our sensibilities and lose the power to discern right from wrong.

But what is background to one may be foreground to another. When I was a young child I noticed that my grandmother recognized noises I did not even hear. We lived with a shared driveway between her home and ours (something that I am sure would violate the building codes of today), with the neighbor's driveway close on the other side of our home. When Grandma was in our home, she would hear every car come into either driveway, perk up, and say, "That sounded like Uncle Bill just drove in," or, "I wonder if that's Kathy coming back from the store." She seemed to have an internal clock, as well as a finely tuned ear for car engines that told her whose the incoming car should be. And when someone did not return home at the appointed hour, she would call us or call our neighbors to see if everything was all right. The sounds that I attenuated as a young boy were the sounds she depended on to care for us.

The word *sensibility* is not used in the scriptures, but the word, *insensibility* does appear (2 Nephi 2:11) in describing the inability to discern good from evil. We become "past feeling" (1 Nephi 17:45). Others' needs no longer matter. We turn inside ourselves because our ties with others and with God have been weakened or broken. And as we turn inside, we become depressed because our vision has been blurred; we can no longer sense our purpose or direction. But even in these moments of difficulty, God has assured us that he will give us direction and restore our power of discernment if we will simply turn to him (see Alma 26:27). He can discern the intents of our heart, and if our heart is right, we will know the direction we should take, even in our most difficult times.

Because our search for an answer to a question of the heart is always a focused search, the search enhances our discernment. Not only are we drawn to people who can help us most in our search, but we are also drawn to help others in their searches—all through discernment. When we study, discernment helps us find the best sources; when we ponder, discernment opens new understanding to our view; when we pray, discernment helps us interpret God's response; and when we "experiment on the word," discernment helps us see the rightness of our answer. This is why discernment is one of the first and most important fruits of the education of the heart; it affects and is affected by every part of the process. And as we taste its effects, our desire for a deeper discernment grows. As with all fruits of the education of the heart, we never feel slighted for the present measure we have received, but we also never feel that we have obtained enough.

Conclusion

Sensibility is one of the first fruits to emerge as a person begins seeking answers to questions of the heart. In the early stages of our search, we can experience an increase in our ability to perceive something in a new way, to interpret our surroundings with greater accuracy, and to understand something that has been confusing. Just as the surgeon gradually developed a sense of touch that allowed him to detect tiny particles of debris in my son's wound, we can develop our senses in ways that allow us not only to perform tasks that were once impossible, but to comprehend truths that were once hidden from view.

As we study and exercise our faith, our sensibility is again enhanced. We hear with new ears, see with new eyes, and touch with new hands. This can change the way a person interprets an event, just as my grandmother interpreted car engine noise differently than I did as a young boy. As our sensibility develops, we will be less prone to "attenuate" others' requests for help; we will begin to hear as my grandmother heard, in a way that allows us to respond more effectively to those around us. And as we seek guidance in our search, our spiritual senses will become more attuned to the promptings that are still and small, promptings that can "bring things to our remembrance" as well as teach us what we need to know at any given moment.

Watchwords

• Sensibility includes one's capacity to feel sympathy for another human being, to experience charity, and to discern truth from error. It draws simultaneously on thought and love, perception and sincerity, interpretation and action.

• When we engage in a search wholeheartedly, our ability to sense and meet others' needs will increase.

• The sense of touch possessed by a surgeon, potter, or violinist may be viewed as the development of sensibility, particularly as the professional uses the skill to benefit others.

• As with all fruits of the education of the heart, sensibility should neither be the aim of our search, nor be measured by external means. Increased sensibility comes as a gift freely given when one faithfully seeks after truth.

CHAPTER EIGHT

REVERENCE

Religious faith means the dedication of one's whole life "in search, reverence, and service" to the object of one's faith, to the great purpose of life. (Lowell Bennion, 1988, p. 186)

When we pursue a question and conduct our search, we develop a reverence for God's creations, for "place," for others, and for God. This is the natural process of the education of the heart.

REVERENCE FOR GOD'S CREATIONS

When I was eight years old, I went to my friend's house to see if he could play, and when I entered his bedroom, his brother was sitting on the bed crying. I had never seen his older brother cry. He was several years older than my friend and someone I had always looked up to, and there he was on his bed sobbing. We left him in the bedroom and went outside where I asked my friend why his brother was crying so uncontrollably. He told me that his brother's goat had just died. This was a goat that he had nursed from a kid, and now the goat was dead. We called it "Nanny" and we used to pet it when my friend's brother would let us. Because we knew that the goat was one of God's creations, the goat helped us develop a sense of reverence; it was a living thing that had worked its way into our lives. And when it died, we all felt the loss.

Those who live on farms often develop a reverence for God's creations just as we developed a reverence out of our love for Nanny. A short time ago I needed to talk to a seventeen-year-old boy about a church meeting. When I asked his mother if I could chat with him before the meeting, she responded, "Well, why don't you just come down and talk to him while he milks the cows?"

Taking her suggestion, I drove to the farm, located the milking barn, and found my young friend leading the next group of cows into the stalls to be milked. Several cows seemed tense and somewhat uncooperative. My friend looked at me and said, "You better go outside until I get them settled. You're a stranger—they don't know you." I stepped outside the milking stalls and waited for a few minutes until he came to get me. He explained that certain cows reacted negatively to strangers and that he could predict which ones would be upset the most by an intruder. He treated his cows with a sense of reverence, which grew out of daily contact with the animals and his knowledge that these animals were gifts of God.

My father is a farmer at heart, even though he had to wait until retirement to get as close to the soil as he had been in his childhood. Although he has always enjoyed growing vegetables, his most favored plants are straw flowers. He grows a wide variety of these flowers every summer, harvests them, hangs them upside down in the garage to dry, and then spends the winter months preparing and arranging them. And his Parkinson's disease has not slowed his propensity to plant and harvest. In fact, I have wondered if the flowers have actually slowed the progress of the disease. A thing of beauty can help us see beyond our individual difficulties in a way that diminishes not only the pain but the cause of the pain as well.

My wife is as committed a gardener as my father and her father. At one time I thought of gardening as seasonal—something that happened in the spring and summer. But my wife has taught me that it is a year-round endeavor. As soon as the garden is "put to bed" in the late fall, only a few weeks pass before the seed catalogues arrive and planning begins for the next spring. My children have learned that the garden must take precedence at times, that if you wait too long to water or to weed, plants can die or be overtaken. They have learned that hard work can be gratifying. They have gained a reverence, I believe, for the latent power of a seed because as they watch the seeds grow into plants, they are reminded of the source of all life.

When the children of Israel were wandering in the wilderness and could not find food, God sent them manna from heaven. The substance was like a "coriander seed" (Exodus 16:31), which they used to make bread during the forty years they were searching for the promised land. Because the manna fell from heaven and appeared on the morning dew, it is likely that the children of Israel at first had reverence for it, but as time passed and they had nothing else to eat, they gradually grew tired of the manna and longed for "the fish, the cucumbers, and the melons, and the leeks, and the onions, and the garlick" (Numbers 11:15) that they had eaten in Egypt. They not only lost reverence for manna, but lost reverence for its source.

When they thirsted, Moses struck the rock and water flowed out freely. Their thirst had been quenched, but they still "murmured" against Moses for their trials in the wilderness. John reminds us in the New Testament that Christ is the bread of life and the water that is given freely (John 6:31-35), but our present culture, much like the children of Israel, has lost reverence not only for the creations that surround it but for the Creator as well. The more our food is laid before us in sterile display cases or delivered to our door ready to eat, the less it reminds us of our connection with God. When the value of food is measured in dollars instead of taste, the food can lose its savor and cause us to forget that the water and the seeds are gifts from God.

Reverence for place. The education of the heart leads to a greater reverence for "place" and for all living things that make a place sacred. I called my parents last fall and asked them if they would like to go for a drive. I mentioned several possible destinations, some close to their home and others further away. They considered the options and requested that I drive them through a canyon located one block away from their home. As we started our journey, my mother began recounting her experiences in the canyon as a child: she told how her father used to work in the canyon and often stayed overnight; how as a teenage girl she slept overnight in the canyon with her friends ("you could never do that now"); and how as a young child she would sleigh ride in the winter from the top of the canyon all the way to the bottom, a distance of four miles. As my parents looked out the car window, they took delight in the fall leaves covering the mountains on either side of the canyon road. The canyon reminded my parents of their place in the world because the canyon was a place that they revered, a place that though open to the public was private in the meaning it held for each of them.

All cultures and religions have sacred places. For the people of Israel, Mount Sinai and the promised land were such places. Jerusalem is such a place for Jews, as well as for Christians and Muslims. When people designate a place as sacred, they usually build some sort of edifice commemorating the event they reverence. These structures range from modest historical monuments to the world's most impressive buildings. In both the Old and New Testaments, the most sacred of all buildings were temples, places where covenants tied God to his children. Because temples are built to remind us that we are eternal, they are built to last.

After visiting Temple Square in Salt Lake City, a friend who does not consider himself to be religious, said:

> It took forty years to build the Salt Lake Temple; it has foundations made of granite rock that are twelve feet thick; this is a building that was made to last. But what are we building today that is made to last? What are the buildings with the most stone and brick? Which ones have the thickest walls? I will tell you—they are banks. These are the buildings in our current culture that convey solidity, security, and strength. We want everyone to believe that bank walls are impregnable, so we construct them with rock and stone. We want everyone to have faith that their money won't be stolen. Yes, banks are the buildings of today that have replaced the temples of the past. (David Solway, personal communication, August 10, 1993)

Whether the replacements for sacred edifices are banks, amusement parks, or shopping malls, in our culture reverence for place has all but disappeared. We have lost our commitment to build temples that remind us of eternity because we have lost touch with the eternal. Rather than asking questions that will lead us closer to God, we ask questions that will help us obtain the world's goods. And the more we worry about how much is in our pocket, the less we come to reverence the things that money cannot buy—the things that remind us of our place among God's creations, the things of the heart.

REVERENCE FOR OTHERS

The education of the heart not only reminds us of the importance of the living things that surround us, it increases our reverence for one another. As God's children we are the sum of all his creations. We were made in his image and have our being in him. But because we are confronted daily with one another's weaknesses, we often fail to see the divine potential in our "classmates." Seeing this potential more clearly is one of the fruits of the education of the heart.

When I was ready to go into the fourth grade, I was dreading the possibility that I would be assigned to Mrs. Walker's class because she had the reputation of being the strictest teacher in the school. When the class lists were posted, I was happy to see that I had been assigned to another teacher. But while I was completing elementary school, Mrs. Walker was studying to obtain her secondary teaching credential. And when I arrived in my eighth-grade English class, there she was; I could not seem to escape her. However, to my surprise, Mrs. Walker was not the cold-hearted taskmaster she had been made out to be. In fact, I found that her class was one of my favorites. I felt that she knew me better than some of my other teachers and that she listened when I had a comment or suggestion. I asked her one day why she left the fourth grade to teach in a junior high school. She said, "I enjoyed teaching in the fourth grade, but the salary in secondary schools is more than elementary teachers earn, and I needed the extra money."

I was surprised that Mrs. Walker's decision had been based on money because she seemed to be so dedicated to teaching. Then I learned that her husband had been permanently disabled and that her family was totally dependent on her teaching salary for support. I came to know her more as an individual than as a public school teacher, and in the process I gained more than the respect a student typically has for a teacher. Her life became more of a lesson to me than her lectures because I came to understand in a limited way who she really was and what she believed in.

The community that forms in a classroom is not unlike our broader society: a community must be based in trust. I came to trust Mrs. Walker because I came to know something of her life. This kind of trust, closely linked with reverence, is becoming rare in our classrooms, as well as in our neighborhoods. We have replaced it with what might be called a "leveraged trust," the kind of trust that we back with money. This is the kind of trust that requires us to put down earnest money to convince the seller of a home that our intent to buy the home is real, or the kind of trust that requires collateral for a loan, an attorney to guarantee title to a property, three forms of identification to cash a check, or "authorization" before something can be charged to a bank card. With this kind of trust we say to each other in essence, "I will trust you so far as you can prove to me that if you are lying I won't be hurt." It is a trust without reverence, which places more confidence in computerized credit ratings than it does in people.

Some might say that such strategies are necessary in transactions between two parties because almost no one can be trusted. But rather than taking this cynical view, we need to remember the mutually dependent nature of reverence and trust. The more reverence we have for another person and the more trust we give, the more worthy that individual becomes of our reverence. And the more reverence we have for one another, the more reverence we ultimately have for God. Because institutions are collections of people, they are susceptible to these same effects. Thus the less trust we place in institutions, the less worthy they become of our reverence. And the less worthy they become of our reverence, the less they tie us to God.

Our present culture bases its transactions on suspicion rather than on trust, on risk management rather than on reverence. We excuse ourselves for doubting each other's integrity by saying that we are simply protecting one another against each other's bad memory. And while there is nothing inherently wrong with recording agreements, there is something wrong with the hocus pocus that accompanies most of our transactions.

When I was searching for an apartment in Paris, a friend sent me a fax explaining two possibilities and recommended that I select the apartment just outside the city limits. I called the *propriétère*, asked a few questions about the apartment, and indicated my interest in renting from him. When I told him that I would be arriving in Paris two weeks before his apartment would be vacated, he said, "Maybe we can arrange something." During our next phone call, he said, "I have spoken with my wife, and we would like to invite you and your family to stay in our place while you are waiting for the other apartment to vacate. We will be on vacation in Switzerland." His offer surprised me so much that I repeated back to him what he had said in French and asked if I had understood correctly. He confirmed his offer. We had never met each other, and yet he was willing to open his home to my family and me. We never signed a contract; we simply agreed on a rental rate and moved in. I did not assume that he was trying to extort as much money as he could from me, and he did not suspect that I might renege on my commitment; we simply trusted each other.

When it came time to rent an electronic piano for the apartment, the store owner told me that because I was not a permanent resident of Paris, I would need to make the rental in the name of someone who trusted me enough to take the full risk associated with the cost of the piano. I asked the wife of the *propriétère* if she would be willing to assist me, and she agreed without hesitating.

A week later she met me at the music store, armed with her utilities bills, "proof of domicile" papers, personal identity cards, and proof of employment papers required by the store owner. I sat off to the side, much like a teenager whose parents are co-signing a loan for a new car, while the store owner and the *propriétère* completed the transaction. At one point the store owner looked over at her and, pointing to me, said, "As far as the store is concerned we know only you—not the *monsieur* here. It is your risk: if your friend here decides to take the piano on a plane with him when he leaves France, you will have to reimburse us the full amount to replace the piano." My *propriétère* seemed not to acknowledge the store owner's comment because, I believe, her response to our request for help was based on trust rather than on risk.

One reason such trust is so uncommon in our culture today is that our reverence for those who speak for God has declined. One role of a prophet is to call the people to repentance; a prophet often tells us things we do not want to hear. And just as the children of Israel murmured against Moses, so too do we fail to give reverence to those who have spoken for God in ancient times or in our day. We regard nothing as sacred or holy, including prophetic messages. And as our reverence for such messages has declined, so has our ability to revere each other. More important than what Bloom (1987) referred to as the "closing of the American mind" is, in reality, the closing of the American heart. When the sacred loses its power to inspire us, we are left empty and alone, wondering why we have been deserted, when all the while we are the ones who have strayed. The education of the heart opens us to divine messages so that we see the sacred and sense the power in both the message and the message bearer. Our resolve to listen with real intent is strengthened because our ability to see others in their true character is increased.

REVERENCE FOR THE CREATOR

We often associate *fear* with *reverence*. But at first glance the words actually seem to conflict with one another. Reverence is based on trust, while fear usually seems to be based on distrust. Rousseau describes a man "who, when dealing with others, thinks only of himself, and . . . in his understanding of himself, thinks only of others" (Rousseau, 1911, p. 5).

Rousseau is referring to the stereotypical president of the corporation who fears that an underling will rise up one day and rob his position from him, along with all the power and money that go with it. The education of the heart leads us to fear the acceptance of evil, which can cause our spiritual death, not to fear another's ability to take our power or money—or even to cause our physical death. We do not fear being separated from our money or from our titles; we do fear being separated from God, which can occur when we give ourselves to evil rather than to good.

> To the degree that man has evil within him, however little, the being who is supremely good will be an object of fear. But just as truly, to the degree that man has goodness in him, however little, the being who is supremely good will be an object of love.
>
> For man in his present state both attitudes are essential. Fear of the Lord dissolves vanity; love of the Lord creates humility. Working together the two attitudes can transform the self (Rasmussen, p. 52).

Conclusion

When people lose faith in the institutions that touch their lives most directly, they lose reverence for everything. If one cannot trust a government leader or even a church leader, why should one have respect for a neighbor? America is famous for constantly mocking its most important institutions. We are confronted daily with a barrage of titillating information about the private lives of everyone from the president to the local priest. And even though the alleged sins are as old as Babylon, the collective effect on our senses often goes unnoticed. We have come to expect the worst of strangers: instead of Communists behind every bush, there are now muggers and molesters in every doorway.

The European loss of faith in their institutional churches seems at times to border on contempt. Many have stories about how their church hurt them or their family at some point in the past. And their feelings are often directed not only at their own church but at religion in general. The reformation may have changed the external practices of churches, but it did little to change the internal reactions of the membership. And the cumulative effect of disintegrating religious faith has been a loss of reverence—not only for God but for all creation.

In our schools we try to approach the quality of reverence (although we would never call it *reverence*) by teaching students to respect one another's rights, to speak when called upon, to take turns, to care for the building, to care for the environment. But reverence goes much deeper; it causes us to see God and his creations with new eyes. It causes us to see the sacredness of human relationships, the beauty of our link with the world, and our oneness with truth. When we act out of reverence we are not acting out of legal duty, we are not even acting strictly out of moral obligation; rather, we are acting out of a love that comes from knowing that all life is sacred. We see the highest in one another when we are filled with reverence—not that we naïvely overlook human frailties, but that we focus on our eternal potential.

To formulate a question of the heart is a reverent act. To form the right question we must recognize the beauty and richness of God's creations, our place in the universe, and the possibility of finding answers. My ethnobotanist friend has a reverence for the native herbal doctors, the plants of Samoa, and the scientific truths that lie in wait to bring the needed benefits to those who suffer. Much of his work must be forming the right question when he meets with the native doctors, when he examines the plants they bring to him, and when he tries to match a plant's healing power with a real human need. In each case, he must approach the task reverently, never allowing his own needs as a scientist to obscure the pathway to truth.

As we study and exercise our faith, our reverence for the topic of our study deepens. We realize that we are not alone in our search, that others have pursued similar questions before us, and that others will continue the search after us. When we ponder and pray, our reverence for God expands. We sense his presence as we listen and keep watch. As our understanding deepens so does our reverence for the one who understands all things. And as we receive guidance, our reverence for our guide increases, a reverence that always ties us closer to God. In the education of the heart, reverence reminds us that seeking truth is a sacred act. A friend recently left a note on my desk with the following quote:

> Gaining knowledge is not like the commonplace work of earning a livelihood. To invade the domain of intelligence, we must approach it as Moses came to the burning bush: we stand on holy ground: we would acquire things sacred: we seek to make our own the attributes of Deity. We must come to this quest of truth—*in all regions of human knowledge whatsoever*—not only in reverence but with the spirit of worship (J. Reuben Clark, 1946, p. 14).

Watchwords

• One develops a reverence for God by sensing reverence for God's creations. The more we remember the source of all life, the more we will live in reverence, and the more our learning will lead us to truth.

• The education of the heart can occur wherever and whenever a learner faithfully seeks truth. However, God has provided certain sacred places (e.g., temples) where one can learn not only about earthly things, but about the things of heaven. We must constantly retain a reverence for such places and make certain that some of our learning occurs there.

• When one has reverence for another person, mutual trust develops. This trust leads to relationships that strengthen our sense of community and increase our reverence for God.

• Reverence replaces fear of God as goodness overcomes evil and we begin to "see with new eyes."

• Seeking answers to questions of the heart is a reverent act. The closer we get to the answer, the nearer we come to the one who embodies all truth.

CHAPTER NINE

HUMILITY

O my son, I desire that ye should deny the justice of God no more. Do not endeavor to excuse yourself in the least point because of your sins, by denying the justice of God; but do you let the justice of God, and his mercy, and his long-suffering have full sway in your heart; and let it bring you down to the dust in humility. (Alma 42:30)

When my daughter Emily was sixteen years old, she had a quarter inch of bone removed from her upper jaw so that her mouth would close normally. The surgery was long and the recovery painful. I remember staying the night with her in the hospital following the operation. As the effects of the anesthetic wore off, she became nauseated and was unable to sleep the entire night. As a result of the surgery her face swelled significantly. When her friends came to visit her the next day, they tried to be cheerful, but the shock in their eyes at seeing Emily's swollen face was hard to disguise.

After returning home, Emily had more friends come to visit, and each time they came I noticed how difficult it was for them to see Emily in such a condition. Although the surgeon had warned her that her face might not return to its normal size for up to one year following surgery, we still felt a sort of sympathetic pain each time we looked at her. And even after the swelling began to decrease, her appearance had changed so much that many friends and extended family members did not recognize her. Some would walk past her in the hallway without saying hello; others would look twice and then say, "Emily, is that you?"

Through the physical pain of the operation and the suffering that followed, Emily learned patience, meekness, and humility. She learned that she had almost no control over her recovery time;

she simply had to wait until her body healed. She learned to submit to doctors, nurses, parents, and God. At times during the night after the surgery she wondered if she would survive the ordeal. She experienced a level of pain she had never before encountered, and she feared at moments that it would not end. At these moments of deepest distress, her "heart was tender, and [she did] humble [her]self before God" (2 Chronicles 34:27).

These experiences taught her that submission was necessary if she wanted to be healed, even when she did not feel like following the "doctor's orders." In the process she learned something that few at the age of sixteen are able to understand—that submitting to those "in authority" (such as parents, physicians, and teachers) is not a sign of personal weakness, but may actually be essential if one is to continue living.

SUBMISSION

Most think of *meekness* or *submissiveness* as signs of weakness: the student who says nothing to a teacher's unjust accusation, or the battered wife who accepts abuse as a way of life. In western culture we want people to "stand up for their rights," to defend themselves when attacked, and to "take control" rather than to "submit"—which we equate with *giving in*. Independence is often seen as the opposite of submission. We value challenging a law and changing it more highly than submitting to the law. Some might assume that if everyone were humble and submissive, the injustices and oppressions that plague our world would never be overcome. Rather than challenge an obvious injustice, all would salute a superior regardless of evil intents or potentially disastrous results.

The holocaust forces us to look at the darker side of submission, raising questions for most observers: Why did Hitler's underlings keep submitting to the inhuman orders of their superiors? Why didn't someone revolt from the inside and stop the massacre of millions of innocent Jews? Was the real enemy an evil tyrant, or was it wholesale *submission* to *authority*? Why didn't those who were taking the orders think more critically, more independently?

Questions of submission are always with us. We realize that society cannot stay intact unless citizens agree to submit to certain laws of conduct, but we recognize at the same moment that if we submit to an unjust law, we have not only weakened ourselves as individuals, but we have weakened our society as a whole. Everyone has struggled with obedience to a law or to a social custom that seems wrong or at least uncomfortable.

Most have felt the pain of compromising personal principles to stay in conformity with a rule or law that contradicted their own moral code. For that very reason, we wonder how the Nazi soldiers could have carried out their grim tasks without personally revolting. Some of the accounts of the holocaust lead us to believe that the perpetrators came to a point where they did not see their acts as moral or immoral; their goal was to accomplish their assigned tasks as completely and as quickly as possible. Rudolf Höss, the chief Nazi officer in charge of the Auschwitz extermination camp, describes in his diary how he simply obeyed orders without allowing himself to reflect on the moral implications of his behavior:

> The reasons behind the extermination programme *seemed to me right. I did not reflect on it at the time;* I had been given an order, and I had to carry it out. Whether this mass extermination of the Jews was necessary or not was something on which I could not allow myself to form an opinion, for I lacked the necessary breadth of view. (Höss, 1991, p. 68, italics added)

From such accounts, we must conclude that there is more than one type of submission, that some types of submission are unhealthy and can lead to the kind of destruction that Höss perpetrated while others are healthy and can lead to the development of humility. I suggest that there are two types of desirable submission that will lead us to wholeness rather than to destruction—

both as individuals and as members of the human family. The first type is "submitting *in* truth;" the second, "submitting *to* truth." These are the ingredients of the education of the heart that bring humility.

Submitting *in* truth. When we submit *in* truth, we open ourselves to truth's invitation; we search humbly and pray faithfully, knowing that truth will find us. Such submission is not a sign of weakness but a sign of conviction and strength because we are submitting voluntarily to an invitation, not involuntarily to an edict. The only way to find truth is to give ourselves to it, and the only way to give ourselves to truth is to place others' needs above our own. When we submit in truth, we extend our hand honestly to those who need us, responding to truth's invitation to give our all, asking nothing in return.

We never submit in truth to a tyrant; one who would oppress us may receive our compliance but never our willing obedience, our attention but never our full devotion. Although prisoners of war may follow the directions of a terrorist guard, they never submit in truth; they never respond to oppression with their heart. While onlookers might describe their outward behavior as submissive, the prisoners are inwardly rejecting everything their oppressors stand for. This is one time when integrity requires that behavior and belief be in opposition.

When we submit in truth, we listen in wholeness. We understand the words and actions of another person because we are able to look at the world through the other's eyes. We forget our own need to feel competent and in control as we willingly subject ourselves to the unfamiliar and the uncomfortable. Learning a foreign language is a case in point. In 1987 six graduate students traveled to Beijing with me to assist Chinese special educators in using computers in their schools. Zhou Lian, a Chinese graduate student who had studied for four years in the U.S., assisted me at Beijing Number One School for the Deaf. In addition to her native Chinese, she spoke very good English. Although I knew some American Sign Language, neither of us could sign in

Chinese. On the second day, while trying to help a profoundly deaf Chinese student use a new piece of software, Zhou Lian came to me feeling both embarrassed and frustrated.

"When the student didn't understand what I was trying to tell him in Chinese," she admitted, "I started speaking English to him. How could I be so stupid? I know he doesn't speak any English—but *I* don't know how to sign to him!"

Although she did not realize it at the time, Zhou Lian was submitting herself to the student—trying to do everything she could to make communication happen. She listened to the student as intently as she could and then tried mightily to help him. In her attempt to communicate, she resorted to something illogical because logic does not always prevail when we are dealing with the unfamiliar, or when we are genuinely trying to help another person—when we are submitting to another's needs rather than trying to meet our own selfish desires.

Trying to master another language is a forceful reminder that learning requires submission—submission to the native speaker's words, grammar, accent, idioms, and even customs. Without such submission, the foreigner can never communicate effectively with the native. However, as with all learning that is part of the education of the heart, the native speaker (the teacher) must also submit to the foreigner (the student). The native must submit to the foreigner's words, grammar, accent, idioms, and customs—at times filling in the blanks for the foreigner, helping the foreigner find the right words and pronunciation. If either one is unwilling to submit, communication (learning) will likely not occur. If both are willing to submit, communication (learning) will occur regardless of the foreigner's level of language mastery.

However, communication and learning cease when either person resolutely decides not to submit. Before our recent stay in France, many warned my family and me about how intolerant Parisians are of Americans. One said, "If you can't speak their language perfectly, you'd better not speak it at all. They'll catch every mistake you make and get angry at you for making it." However, rather than finding arrogance, we found kindness; rather than intolerance, acceptance.

I have asked myself why such negative stereotypes develop and endure. Is the American who expects all French people to understand English actually the arrogant one? Could the stereotype—and all negative stereotypes for that matter—be traced back to a lack of willingness to submit to one another as learners and teachers?

I once asked a Chinese graduate student to participate more in class and be willing to voice her disagreements when she had an alternative point of view. In one sense, I was helping her to adjust to the norms of American higher education, as the Chinese culture discourages student questioning and participation, but I was also imposing my cultural values on her. I was asking that she think for herself and voice her criticisms like American students. Although my advice was well intended, I am now convinced that I should have approached the problem in another way. Had I submitted myself more to her needs, rather than trying to make her over in the image of an American student, we both could have learned more effectively.

In her book *Peripheral Visions,* Mary Catherine Bateson (1994) admits that "we may not use the word *humility,* but it is becoming important to recognize new kinds of fluidity and openness to learning at every stage of the life cycle, in home, school, and workplace" (p. 74). When I read this passage, I wondered why we avoid the word *humility.* Why do we prefer words like *fluidity* and *openness* or *self-esteem* and *critical thinking?* Why do we believe that critical thinking, for example, is more important than submitting in truth? Do we discourage students from experiencing the kind of learning that leads to the education of the heart when we teach them that their most important role is to challenge, to criticize, to dissect someone else's thought in order to illuminate inaccuracies or inadequacies? Can a person be humble and critical at the same moment?

We have all seen examples of those who have developed one trait without the other. The Sadducees and Pharisees, for instance, were critical but not humble. They were learned, had high self-esteem (see Luke 18:11), and were quick to point out Christ's deviations from accepted ecclesiastical practice (see Luke 7:9). They were masterful critics but had lost their sense of the sacred. Rather than submitting in truth to the unfamiliar teachings of Christ, they held onto their traditional rule books so they could maintain control. They believed that by opening themselves to Christ's teachings, they would lose status in the eyes of the people; and so they failed to recognize that the eyes of God were upon them. Rather than asking questions of the heart, they asked questions of trickery and sarcasm, always trying to catch Jesus in an infraction of traditional law (see, for example, Matthew 9:11).

The Sadducees and Pharisees demonstrate that education must have a higher aim than teaching students to think critically or raising students' self-esteem. In the education of the heart, humility replaces self-esteem and discernment replaces critical thinking as the fundamental fruits that come from seeking truth. Thus rather than trying to be humble and *critical* at the same moment, those who experience the education of the heart learn to be humble and discerning. In this way, when we submit ourselves in truth, we recognize truth when it knocks.

Submitting *to* truth. When we submit ourselves to truth, we recognize it, give thanks for it, and embrace it. We allow truth to enter our heart, to take root in our soul, and to change us. We see beauty and goodness in the small and simple things that surround us, beauty and goodness that were once hidden from our view. And because we see anew, we respond differently to those who cross our path. In the process, we must usually give up some former way of thinking or acting because when "old things are done away, all . . . become new" (3 Nephi 12:47).

When the disciples accepted Jesus as the embodiment of all truth, they each gave up their vocations to serve him. They left their old way of life behind and went on to a new way. Submitting to truth is always a process of renewal, a process that is abundantly evident in the early years of a child's life and sometimes seems to disappear from the lives of adults. Children explore, experiment, and discover—all without expecting anything in return. Surprise is one of the most common ways children learn because they are usually unable to predict the result of their actions. They learn by discovery that putting a glass on the edge of a table can lead to a broken glass and that placing a heavy object on the top of a stack of blocks can cause the whole tower to topple. But as adults, we pride ourselves in our ability to predict how things will turn out. We say to ourselves, "We are experienced; we know how things work." And the more we convince ourselves of our predictive powers, the less we are able to experience learning through surprise and renewal.

Submitting to truth often requires that we accept surprise when it comes. When my youngest daughter, Lisa, was eleven years old, we were returning from Washington, D.C., when the pilot announced that because of unfavorable weather the plane would need to land in Indianapolis rather than in Chicago, the intended destination. He explained that we would wait on the ground in Indianapolis until he received further instructions from the Chicago airport. Two men seated in front of my daughter and me immediately began to complain about the airline. "Don't they read the weather report before they take off? We should have stayed in D.C. instead of wasting our time on the ground in Indiana!" they remarked.

I could not help but contrast the reaction of my daughter with that of the two gentlemen in front of us. As soon as she heard the pilot's announcement, she turned to me and exulted, "Oh, that means we'll get to go to another city! I've never been to Indianapolis before!" She pointed to the phone attached to the seat back ahead of us. "Can I use the 'airphone' to call Mom and tell her that we'll be late?"

It seemed the longer we sat on the tarmac in Indiana, the more enjoyable it was for my daughter, and the more frustrating it was for the men in front of us. She enjoyed looking out the window at the sunset; the men in front of us never noticed that the sun went down. She liked the extra food and drinks the flight attendants brought to us; the men complained about the tastelessness. She submitted herself to the surprise landing in Indiana; the men fought it because from their perspective the surprise stole some of their control and their ability to predict the future. My daughter learned how far Indianapolis was from Chicago, how to use an airphone, and how to interpret the messages sent from the control tower to the pilot as she listened with her headset. The two gentlemen, like so many "educated" adults, learned little because they had forgotten how to submit themselves to an unexpected situation.

When we submit ourselves to truth, the unfamiliar takes on meaning and the uncomfortable begins to feel like home. At the beginning of their search for a cure to ALD, the Odones were intimidated by the scientific and medical worlds they had to face. The new scientific terms, the federal regulations, and the traditions of the ALD parent association were foreign and frustrating. But as they searched for answers, the terms became *their* terms, the regulations and traditions became part of the search process rather than insurmountable roadblocks. By the end of the search, the Odones had written scientific papers on ALD that prominent scientists and physicians were reading. And they created their own associations to carry on the search for answers to the continuing questions about the disease.

Anyone who submits to truth is strengthened, not weakened, because God-given gifts are magnified. Gifts of discernment, reverence, and charity are all intensified when we submit to truth, making it possible for the humble person to strengthen others by serving them. Rather than losing a sense of identity, those who submit to truth recognize more clearly than ever their eternal nature. The most humble of all knew who he was and understood his mission. He was submissive and meek, and yet he was all-powerful. As Rousseau has said,

> The first step in escaping our misery is to recognize it. Let us be humble in order to be wise; let us admit our weakness and

we will be strong.*(Le premier pas pour sortir de notre misère est de la connaître. Soyons humbles pour être sages; voyons notre faiblesse, et nous serons forts.)* (Lettre VI (Robert, 1988, p. 280)

Conclusion

It is not popular to be humble. As a culture we seek more to be assertive than submissive, authoritative than meek, and efficient than kind. As a virtue, humility has simply fallen out of fashion. Parents, teachers, professional counselors, and church leaders usually worry more about a person's self-esteem than they do about a person's humility. Many see self-esteem as the key to personal happiness.

On the surface, self-esteem seems like a positive attribute. Its promoters believe that high self-esteem is a prerequisite for a full and happy life because, they say, only when people understand their full potential will they be able to reach it. The promoters point to those who suffer from depression or other psychological maladies and conclude that if their self-esteem were higher, their maladies could be cured or avoided altogether. Self-esteem is portrayed as a powerful preventative medicine for the mind. For many teachers, counselors, and parents, self-esteem becomes the touch point, the personal quality that is most worthy of attention. They see it as the key to learning (because when students have confidence in their abilities, they can attack new learning tasks successfully), as well as to interpersonal relationships (because only when children feel "good about themselves" can they learn to love others). Self-esteem may have replaced humility as a central human virtue.

When a culture replaces humility with self-esteem, there is a danger that its members will become increasingly self-conscious, self-satisfied, and self-indulgent. The harder we work on "self-awareness," the less we understand our place in the world and in eternity. Intentionally trying to "find ourselves" is like trying to capture our likeness by painting over the image staring back at us in the mirror: the more we paint, the less we can see our actual image.

Without some measure of humility one cannot experience the education of the heart, but as one questions and searches, humility will always deepen. To ask a question of the heart, we must recognize our lack of wisdom, and we find that the more we learn, the more we sense how unlearned we really are. As a colleague said, "Just when we think we have understood something, it is like walking up to the edge of the sea and looking out at the vastness of the waters yet to be explored." We recognize that competence is not our ultimate goal because competence is a fleeting illusion. We can never allow ourselves to think that we have "arrived." Thus, the more we explore, the more we question, and the more we question, the more we recognize we do not know. This is why a question of the heart that grows out of humility can humble us even further because most answers do not come easily, and the answers we do obtain help us to sense our place in the infinite expanse of God's creations.

When we study and exercise our faith, we again are struck with our inadequacies, our inability to find truth on our own. Without humility one does not engage in such study. But there is a big difference between humbly submitting ourselves to those who assist us in our search and hiring others to provide us with data so that we can answer questions that have been imposed on us. The corporate officer who orders an underling to produce a series of graphs showing last quarter's performance without conviction of its value will likely not become more humble in the process; neither will the underling. Neither will the teacher who assigns students to complete a worksheet—not because she is convinced of its value but simply because it is part of the state core curriculum—become more humble in the process; nor will the student.

The teacher and the learner who humble themselves will ponder and pray about what they are attempting to learn and to teach. They will seek guidance from others and from God, and as they seek such guidance, they will be humbled by the answers they receive. The teacher should be viewed as a seeker of truth, along with the learner, as one who is willing to submit in truth and submit to truth. Such a view, I am convinced, would cause us all to learn differently and to teach differently. If we approached learning and teaching in humility, yielding ourselves to each other and to God, we would eventually come to see one another as humble guides who easily change from teacher to learner because we would have no fear of losing status or identity, no fear "of belonging to another, or to others, or to God." We would be free to search. And "the only wisdom we [would] hope to acquire [would be] the wisdom of humility: humility is endless" (T. S. Eliot, in King & Warner, 1990, p. 500).

Watchwords

• Humility requires righteous submission. When we submit in truth, we open ourselves to truth's invitation, listen for its call, and study faithfully. When we submit to truth, we embrace it as it embraces us, allowing it to change us just as the disciples were changed when they gave up their former ways and followed the Savior.

• Humble people may have faith in their ability to do "good and great things," but they do not seek to improve their self-esteem or become more self-actualized. Rather than complaining that their own needs are not being met, they seek constantly to meet the needs of others.

• Without humility, one will not engage in a search for answers to questions of the heart; thus, humility is both a prerequisite for and a fruit of such learning.

• When we humbly seek after truth, we will be protected from submitting to unrighteous demands that might be placed upon us. We will know how to respond to such demands in ways that benefit rather than injure those around us.

CHAPTER TEN

EDIFICATION

And that which doth not edify is not of God, and is darkness.
(Doctrine & Covenants 50:23)

Let us therefore follow after the things which make for peace, and things wherewith one may edify another. (Romans 14:19)

Edification is different from the other fruits of the education of the heart: it is a communal process. We might sense the other fruits of the education of the heart in privacy, but we experience edification *together.* We might do or say something that edifies someone else; another person might edify us. We might be edified by a sacred text—but even then, the author himself edifies us, not the pages upon which the words are written.

When I was a Church adviser to a group of young men, I invited each twelve- and thirteen-year-old boy to follow the counsel of Gordon B. Hinckley (president of the LDS Church) to memorize the thirteenth section of the Doctrine and Covenants, the account of the restoration of the Aaronic Priesthood. At that time, President Hinckley was serving as a counselor to then-President Spencer W. Kimball. The young men were able to memorize the verse with such ease that I invited them to commit other scriptures to memory. After a period of several months, most of them had learned to recite at least six scriptures, and all of them could say the thirteenth section with few pauses. Wondering if President Hinckley, a former neighbor, would like to hear the "fruits" of his counsel, I called his secretary and asked if he might be able to spare "ten minutes" for the young men to visit him. After speaking with him, his secretary called me back to say that he would be happy to see us.

One afternoon following school, all twenty-two boys piled

into several cars and traveled from Provo to LDS Church head-quarters in Salt Lake City. President Hinckley welcomed us into his office and invited us to follow him into a room with a large conference table and a world globe in the corner. After we had each found a seat, he pointed to the globe and said, "You know, young men, I have greeted many people in this room who have come from all over the world. Presidents of the United States have sat with me in this room where you're sitting now." The boys' eyes got bigger.

He was in no hurry to hear us recite our scriptures but continued talking with the boys as if he had known them for years. And for some reason they seemed to be listening to him more intently than they usually did in Sunday meetings. Finally, he said, "I understand that you can recite the thirteenth section of the Doctrine and Covenants." At that point I motioned to a thirteen-year-old boy, who was seated at the opposite end of the long conference table, to take charge and lead the young men in reciting the scripture. He stood and invited the boys to join him in reciting the thirteenth section. President Hinckley mouthed every word as the young men went through the verse, and when they were finished, he congratulated them. But they responded, "We have more scriptures we want to say for you."

The boys proceeded to recite Mosiah 4:30, John 3:16, Moses 1:39, Moroni 7:47, and Doctrine and Covenants 20:58-59. I noticed that President Hinckley, although he had no warning about which verses we would recite, again mouthed every word with the boys. He was surprised and pleased that they had gone beyond his counsel and had memorized more than just the one verse. After the boys had recited all of their scriptures, President Hinckley just looked back with a smile and asked, "Tell me, how long did it take you to memorize all these scriptures?" He continued by expressing his pleasure at hearing them recite the verses and then invited them to ask questions. He spent far longer than the ten minutes I had originally requested. The boys knew they had experienced something that they would not soon forget.

As I have reflected on what happened that day sitting around the conference table, I have concluded that the boys, the adult advisers, and President Hinckley all experienced edification. When scriptures are recited together, "all are edified." This is the type of teaching and learning we seek in the education of the heart, a time when everyone who is together is lifted and is brought closer to Deity. Edification is a feeling that is difficult to describe but easy to recognize—particularly as we gain more experience with it. These boys were beginning to gain that kind of experience.

As with all fruits of the education of the heart, edification is not bound by time or space; its effects multiply as the years pass. My son, who was one of the twenty-two boys who visited President Hinckley that day, has told me that the scriptures he learned as a boy were the ones he relied on most heavily seven years later as an LDS missionary in Montréal, Québec. He describes how he used them to prepare talks and to teach investigators. He was drawing upon edification he had received as a boy to edify others as he served a mission. Edification is thus a communal process; when one is strengthened, the necessary thing to do is to strengthen another.

EDIFICATION IN THE HOME

Although she would not use the word to describe herself, my wife's mother is an expert in edification. It is impossible to be around her for even a few minutes without feeling more capable, more prepared to face the future. She knows how to strengthen those she loves. Her efforts to edify are never forced or feigned; she exults in every accomplishment of every family member. She sincerely knows that one child will be "the best student in the whole school," another "the best jumping center who ever played basketball," and another "the best musician who ever lived—the budding Bach or Beethoven." She builds up her family members by dwelling on what they are doing with their lives at the moment; she strengthens them by focusing on their strengths.

When we visit my wife's parents, who are now in their nineties, my wife's mother always asks the children, "Have you been a good girl (or boy)? Open your mouth so I can see inside." She then gives each mouth a thorough examination, and as she looks inside, she voices her diagnosis: "Oh, I can tell you've been good." As she comments, she waits for the child to confirm each remark, and then she says, "I *knew* you'd been good; I can always tell." When the children were young they looked forward to these "grandma exams" as part of the ritual of visiting their grandparents. They knew that they would somehow feel better after she had looked in their mouths and told them what she could see. The children never questioned the need for their grandma to look inside their mouths to see if they had been "good"; it seemed natural, I believe, that their grandma would not be able to discern their goodness solely by examining their outward appearance.

This kind of edification is part of the education of the heart. It is personal, coming from one who knows us and is invested in us; it grows not out of policy or regulation, but out of love.

THE MEANING OF THE WORD *EDIFY*

The first meaning of the word *edify* is "to build or construct." The French verb *edifier* is used much like the verb *erect* in English—to construct a building. But the second meaning of the word focuses more on the function of spiritual strengthening, drawing a person closer to "virtue." Briefly stated, to *edify* means "to build up the soul" (Simpson & Weinere, 1989, p. 71). It is an essential fruit of the education of the heart. And while some might argue about what it means to build up the soul, my wife's mother, and others like her, will go on edifying those around them.

ENTERTAINMENT OR EDIFICATION

As our culture has replaced humility with self-esteem, so have we replaced edification with entertainment. Television, movies, and computer-games have taken the place of reading good literature, listening to good music, and appreciating good art. To succeed in the children's market, these media must *excite* the viewer by including some type of violence; to succeed in the adult market, the television program or movie must *titillate* the viewer by including vulgar language, nudity, or graphic sexual content. The movie rating scale itself is nothing more than a scale of pornography: the further one moves along the scale, the more pornographic the content becomes. Script writers and movie producers have made a science out of "working around" the rating system so that they can produce a movie that will contain just the right amount of offensive material in order to merit a PG, a PG-13, or an R rating—all of this in the name of free speech.

Saying that citizens have the right to choose pornography because they prefer that type of entertainment is like saying that citizens have the right to choose open sewage because they prefer that type of waste disposal system. When either pornographic entertainment or open sewage waste disposal become acceptable, everyone in the culture suffers from its ill effects. Just as whole societies grow accustomed to a water supply that is not fit to drink, we have grown accustomed to images that are not fit to view and sounds that are not fit to hear. Rap music that encourages listeners to kill police officers; stand-up comedy that replaces healthy humor with lewd language and gestures; movies, magazines, and videos, and now compact discs, filled with nudity and sex—these are the dark signs of a society that has replaced edification with a kind of entertainment that subtly dulls our sensibilities, resulting in a disease of the heart and of the soul.

Instead of fighting this negative trend toward entertainment, our schools often embrace it. Rather than aiming for instruction that edifies, our schools frequently yield to current custom. Many have forgotten that cultural acceptance of a behavior does not mean that the behavior is right or good. Neither cheating on a test nor cheating on a spouse is more morally acceptable today than it was a half-century ago when such behavior was less prevalent. And yet we look the other way when students cheat, and schools dispense condoms so that "sexually active" students will infect or impregnate each other less frequently, even though it has been shown that such practices are ineffective at reducing either teenage pregnancy or the spread of AIDS (see Whitehead, B. D., 1994).

A society that tolerates cheating, that accepts promiscuity, or that permits verbal or physical abuse cannot edify anyone. For this reason the lives parents and teachers live are far more important in teaching than are textbooks in the schools or tax code documents in governments. If a student learns in a human biology course that abstinence "has advantages" and is then offered condoms on the way out of the school door, the lesson on abstinence evaporates. Likewise, if a parent tells a child to be honest and then cheats on a tax return, the lesson on honesty will eventually mean nothing.

When we teach in our schools or in our homes, we believe that we must "gain attention," and "motivate," and "energize," but we seldom think about what it means to edify. To edify means to help someone approach virtue, and many are afraid to teach children and youth what it means to be good. My wife's mother once taught in what would now be called an "alternative high school"—a school for students who did not survive in the regular system. Decades later she still enjoys telling how she taught some of these students to read when they were sixteen and seventeen years old and how she had them correct their own tests. "They always gave themselves two marks on each test," she recounts. "One was for the percentage of items they got right, and the other was for honesty. I always taught them that it was much more important to get an 'A' in honesty than it was to get 100% correct on the test."

Edification not only draws us closer to virtue, it helps us face our daily challenges with more strength and faith. President Hinckley's counsel to the boys strengthened them twice: first as he encouraged them to memorize the scripture, and next as he congratulated them on their successful completion of the task. I believe that his encouragement as we were sitting around the conference table gave the boys renewed energy and commitment to carry on with their memorization. When respected adults recognize a child's success, as President Hinckley or my wife's mother did, the child is fortified. Edification thus builds faith both in the "speaker" and the "listener." It helps bind us to one another as it binds us to God, expanding our capacity to attack unfamiliar problems, learn what we need to learn, and repent of past errors.

INTENTIONAL EDIFICATION

Unlike other fruits of the education of the heart, edification is often intentional. Just as my wife's mother taught her students to be honest, a family can plan to read scriptures together, a leader can deliver an edifying speech to members of the organization, or an artist can create a work of beauty. When Christ gave the Sermon on the Mount, he intended to edify those who would listen and follow. When Paul wrote letters to the Ephesians, he intended to strengthen and build the members of the church in that city. Christ's messages, as well as Paul's, were always intended to edify. Their messages were not always easy to receive; they often caused the recipient to give up a way of thinking or behaving and replace it with a new way, but they always carried the humble disciple closer to virtue.

During a visit to a French maternal school, I watched as a teacher read French poetry to a group of five-year-olds. She spoke in whispered tones as she prepared the children to listen to a poem entitled, "The Secret." She kept whispering as she began reciting the poem from memory, motioning with her hands for each student to watch and listen carefully. Spellbound by her recitation, the children leaned forward on their seats so they could hear every word and see every expression on the teacher's face. As soon as she had finished, one of the children said, "Now will you read the one in the red book—the one you read yesterday?" The teacher, somewhat surprised at the request, looked over at me and said, "I'm surprised he would remember which book this poem was in; yesterday was the first time I've ever read from that book."

The boy delighted in every word of the poem, and when he asked to hear it again, the teacher said, "Instead of reading it again right now, I'll help you make a poster with the poem on it; you can paint a picture on it and take it home and hang it on the wall so you can see it every day. Someday you'll be able to read every word of the poem, but in the meantime your parents can help you with the words." The boy was satisfied.

The teacher continued to recite one poem after another, sometimes completely from memory, other times looking at the page periodically for a cue. She read a humorous poem about impossible events, each line ending with *"Ça n'existe pas, Ça n'existe pas"* ("That just couldn't be, That just couldn't be"). The children waited for these lines at the end of each stanza so they could repeat them with the teacher and laugh at the absurdity of the images that came to their minds. They wanted to hear the poem again and again. Instead, the teacher began to explain that while some poems were funny, some were sad, as well. She then read a poem entitled, "The King Is Sad," which told the story of a king who had lost a loved one and how no amount of money or fame could soothe the pain of his loss.

As I watched and listened, I wondered how many teachers in America were reading poems to their students at the same moment. I could imagine many singing songs with young children, but I doubted that many were sharing poems with their students—poems that they had learned by heart. And by laying aside this part of learning, teachers cause students to miss out on the kind of edification that these young French children were receiving—a kind of edification that comes from words that are joined together in ways that remind us that life is sacred and that learning can be sacred too. I wondered about how different education would be if we could eliminate the lewd and vulgar language of the media and the flat and uninspired language of school texts and replace them with the language of poetry.

UNINTENTIONAL EDIFICATION

Regardless of how much a teacher, parent, or leader prepares to edify, the unpredictable events that bring life to the teaching will often be more edifying than the events that were planned. Although the French teacher planned to read poetry to her children, she did not plan in advance to prepare a poster with the boy's favorite poem so he could share it with his family. Neither did she know in advance which poems the children would request. Because every good teacher has experienced the benefits of spontaneous student comments, some conclude that all planning is counterproductive, that instruction should just happen. But spontaneity is predicated more upon prior preparation than on a planned lesson because teachers are then freer to pursue the unpredictable question when they have pursued similar questions on their own.

With some, it is not so much what they intend to teach that edifies us, it is simply their presence. At times we are edified by a casual encounter with a friend or by a family member who visits us when we are recovering from an illness. This type of edification can literally heal us—both spiritually and physically. While observing patients in a critical care unit, James J. Lynch, a medical researcher, noticed that abnormally high heart rates declined when family members walked into the room, and particularly when they touched the patient (Lynch, 1979). The more he observed, the more clearly he saw what was happening—healing occurred more readily when loved ones visited and cared for the patient. He began to wonder how pervasive the effect was. "What influence does the presence of family members have on a patient's ability to recover?" he asked himself. His study led him to examine mortality data that showed that patients who have no close family members have higher mortality rates for virtually every major cause of death (heart disease, cancer, liver disease, and suicide, etc.) than do patients who live with loved ones.

The New Testament account of the woman who had been diseased "with an issue of blood for twelve years" reminds us of the power of touch. When the woman touched the hem of Christ's garment, she was healed, and as the healing occurred Christ felt "virtue" go out of him (Luke 8:43-48). Christ's presence prompted the woman to approach him. She knew that Christ's power would heal her, and he assured her that it was her faith that had made her whole. Christ did not plan the event; it happened as he was on his way to serve someone else. He edified others simply by his presence. Christ's healing influence can edify us as it did the woman. We can be made whole by learning and teaching that draw us to him.

Like the critically ill patients, we can also be edified by those we love. And for this kind of edification to occur, all we need is the presence of family members. Even if they are not living among us, they can edify us when we contemplate their life. This is one reason our "hearts turn" to our loved ones who have gone on before us and their hearts turn to us (Doctrine & Covenants 2:2).

My grandmother edifies me regularly as I think about the time she lived among us before her death at ninety-four. She had been widowed at an early age while pregnant with her fifth child. After a serious automobile accident that claimed the life of her son, she experienced a miraculous recovery. To support her children she ironed neighbors' clothes. In today's vernacular she would be called a single mother or a displaced homemaker. But although she remained single following the death of her husband, she never seemed the least bit displaced. She took care of herself and took care of her family. She never held any position of renown in the community and was never accorded any meritorious title, but at the time of her death—even though she had lived a long life and died naturally among family members—hundreds attended her funeral. They came, I believe, because they had all been edified by her presence and wanted to hold on as long as they could to the example that she had left them.

CONDITIONS OF EDIFICATION

Isaiah prophesied that many would draw near to God "with

their mouth, and with their lips," but would "[remove] their hearts far from him" (Isaiah 29:13). We cannot be edified by God or by others unless our heart is right, and our heart is not right until we have received the other fruits of the education of the heart. This is why two people can listen to the same message and respond in completely different ways: one lifted and strengthened, the other bored. Thus the heart of the teacher and the heart of learner must both be right if either is to be edified. And when edification occurs, our heart will again be strengthened; we will feel the flow of virtue into us as the woman felt it flow into her when she touched Christ.

As learners and teachers we must come to know one another if we are to edify each other. I can be edified by someone I know long after I have been separated from the person by distance or by death—but only if I have come to know the person. The sterile dissemination of information that is counted for education in so many universities is not edifying for the teacher or the students because they cannot know one another in classes that enroll hundreds. When my oldest son began taking courses from teachers who knew him and valued his contribution, his outlook on education changed dramatically. He began to look forward to tasks that he had once considered drudgery because he was using what he was learning in class to help professors with their research. He was invited to question and then explore until he found answers. His professors took an interest not only in his work but in him as a person and in his future. He experienced edification.

Conclusion

Edification occurs when we experience any one of the fruits of education of the heart. When our sensibilities are enhanced, our reverence for God and his creations increased, or our humility deepened, we are edified; when we experience inspiration or joy in our learning and teaching, we are likewise edified. Edification is a fruit of education that has been forgotten by most learners and teachers. We seldom expect or plan for it because so much of what passes for education is sterile and lifeless, so much of what we are exposed to daily is cheap and degrading. The education of the heart, however, always lifts, even though it often challenges our present way of thinking and acting.

A good question can be as edifying as a good answer. As a question of the heart captures us, it edifies and fortifies us for the search ahead. It points us in the right direction and focuses our attention. It propels us to search and fuels our search once we have begun. Seldom does such a question edify only the one who poses it; invariably others are drawn in by the question and are equally edified by it.

Effective study is equally edifying. We are lifted, built, and changed by study and faith. We begin to see things differently than we saw them before; we refine our question and refocus our search. At each stage we receive new strength, even when our search does not seem to be yielding the results we anticipated.

Pondering leads to personal discoveries. It allows us to become one with the problem, to get inside it and to let it get inside us, to taste it and sense it. We begin to know what we must do to solve it, how we should approach the next step, and who might help us along the way. Pondering leads us closer to truth, and as we move closer with each step, we are edified. Likewise prayer draws us closer to God, who literally gives us new strength and new faith to continue our search. His guidance edifies us as he gives us "sweet counsel" through the scriptures, through prophets, and through those who have joined us in our search.

We know we are experiencing edification when we are drawn closer to God, better able to confront our challenges, more at peace, and less diverted by the tawdry and titillating things of the world. We see things more clearly, recognize beauty and truth more readily, and sense a greater need to serve those around us. An ancient prophet, Enos, once prayed for forgiveness, but as soon as he felt forgiven, he desired to help others as well:

Behold, I went to hunt beasts in the forests; and the words which I had often heard my father speak concerning eternal life, and the joy of the saints, sunk deep into my heart.

And my soul hungered; and I kneeled down before my Maker, and I cried unto him in mighty prayer and supplication for mine own soul; and all the day long did I cry unto him; yea, and when the night came I did still raise my voice high that it reached the heavens.

And there came a voice unto me, saying: Enos, thy sins are forgiven thee, and thou shalt be blessed. And I, Enos, knew that God could not lie; wherefore, my guilt was swept away.

And I said: Lord, how is it done?

And he said unto me: Because of thy faith in Christ, whom thou hast never before heard nor seen. And many years pass away before he shall manifest himself in the flesh; wherefore, go to, thy faith hath made thee whole. *Now, it came to pass that when I had heard these words I began to feel a desire for the welfare of my brethren, the Nephites; wherefore, I did pour out my whole soul unto God for them.* (Enos 1, italics added)

Like the woman who touched Christ, Enos was healed—not of a physical malady but of a sickness of the soul. His heart was right, he was humble, he reverenced God, and he had the sensibility to know when God spoke peace to his heart. As healing came wholly to him, he sensed the needs of those around him. He knew that many of them were struggling as he had struggled; he knew that some were following a road to destruction. And he wanted to help them. This is the natural fruit of edification.

Watchwords

• Unlike other fruits of the education of the heart, edification is a communal process, something we experience together.

• Edification causes us to feel more capable of facing life's problems because our learning brings us closer to God, the one who is always waiting to "fill our cup when we come to the well."

• One should never be satisfied with entertainment as a substitute for edification. Entertainment, even in its best forms, aims to amuse or delight, while edification uplifts and strengthens us.

• Unlike the other fruits, edification can be both intentional and unintentional. As parents or teachers, we should prepare in ways that will lead to edification for our children and students. But we should also recognize that many of our most edifying moments will come unexpectedly at any point in our search.

CHAPTER ELEVEN

Inspiration

And the Lord God formed man [of] the dust of the ground, and breathed into his nostrils the breath of life; and man became a living soul. (Genesis 2:7)

On a trip around the European continent, my family and I experienced wild variations in air quality. When we left Paris—a city often filled with the kind of pollution that most "modern" cities endure—we were breathing air contaminated with industrial particulates mixed with the carbon monoxide from the exhausts of countless vehicles that spent more time snarled in traffic jams than rolling down the street. As we moved on to other large cities, we noticed that they suffered from the same type of air pollution we had left behind us. Our most difficult moment came while traveling through a tunnel filled with choking exhaust fumes. The smoke was so thick we stopped talking to one another, inhaling as little of the befouled air as possible, waiting impatiently for the end of the tunnel so we could once more find breathable air.

Leaving the large cities behind, we traveled to Denmark, where we saw fewer smokestacks, fewer cars—more trees, more farms, and much more clean air. We enjoyed standing outside, even though it was quite cold, and breathing deeply without any of the choking or burning sensations that came from inhaling the air (if it could be called that) in the tunnel. We were reminded again that the air we were breathing was giving us life—we could feel its renewing power each time we took another breath.

We were reminded that air is the most precious commodity for life; deprived of it for longer than a few minutes, we die. Each time we take a breath of fresh air, we are renewed; if we allow ourselves to become conscious of the process, we sense the life-giving properties of a substance that we can neither see with our eyes nor hold in our hand. Only when we are deprived of it—or when it is mixed with the poisons humans constantly pump into it—do we come to appreciate fresh air.

When God breathed life into Adam, the air was even cleaner than the air we breathed in Denmark. God's air was the breath of life—spiritual air that fused with Adam's body and made him a living soul. The oldest meaning of the word *inspire* is to "breathe or blow upon or into" (Simpson & Weinere, 1989, p. 1037). God literally *inspired* Adam, and at the very moment that God blew life into him, Adam inhaled so that he could receive God's *inspiration*. The second oldest meaning of the word *inspire* is "to draw in breath" (ibid.). Without both actions—God's breath and Adam's inhalation, Adam could not live.

We seldom associate breathing with the word *inspire;* rather we think of what dictionaries call its "theological" meaning: "a special immediate action or influence of the Spirit of God upon the human mind or soul" or more generally infusing "[something] into the mind; to kindle, arouse, awaken in the mind or heart (a feeling, idea, impulse, purpose, etc.)" (ibid.). Prophets are inspired as they write scripture. Artists, writers, and composers are inspired as they create their paintings and sculptures, books and poems, or songs and symphonies. But many of us have forgotten the richness of the word as we use it today to describe an "inspired thought" or an "inspired move on the part of the opponent." We often use the word *inspiration* when we simply mean *intuition*.

In common conversation we are usually more comfortable with words like *intuition* or *insight* to describe the sudden "Aha!" that learners experience than we are with the word *inspiration*. Admitting that people can think intuitively and finding ways to assist the intuitive process are laudable goals, but they do not go far enough. Intuition, in its most commonly accepted sense, is an internal process, a process that points the learner inward. Receiving new insight is similarly something that occurs inside the learner, a mental process that causes the learner to rely on internal resources alone.

Intuition assumes that we can be whole human beings by ourselves; inspiration defines wholeness as being one with God and with others (see *Class Notes, #6*). Unless we admit to a power greater than our own, we cannot be whole. And unless we submit ourselves in faith to that power, we will be forever reduced to a collection of cells, whether we adhere to cognitivism, behaviorism, or any other form of rationalism. Rationalist approaches turn us inward, removing us from God—the one who gave us life and the only one who can make us whole. When we accept God as our creator, we can accept inspiration, a process that is available to all who will make their heart ready to receive it.

Inspiration can remove the limits that we often place on ourselves as learners because we come to understand that we have not been left alone. When inspiration comes, we are drawn closer to what is good, true, and beautiful; we are drawn closer to God because, like Adam, we take in the breath of life and sense it in our whole being. Inspiration is an inevitable fruit of the education of the heart.

SOURCES OF INSPIRATION

To receive inspiration, we must constantly seek its sources, for we will not receive what we do not seek.

God as a source of inspiration. All inspiration ultimately comes from God because God possesses all truth, and truth is what we seek. When we obtain an answer to a question of the heart, the answer comes from God regardless of the immediate sources we come to rely on in our search. As the supreme creator, God breathes the power of creativity into our being. This power inspires us to go forward in faith and do what the Lord would have us do, and it fortifies us in our search. But seldom will we sense inspiration as directly as Adam sensed the breath of life coming from God; rather it will come naturally as we engage in our search with "full purpose of heart."

Scientists, artists, and athletes often use the word inspiration to describe their best work. Even those who do not believe in a god as such describe their best performance as an experience aided from another source—from something outside themselves. Although Noddings and Shore (1984) use the following excerpt from Mozart's writings to explain intuition, I prefer to use it as an example of inspiration, the word the composer himself used to describe the creative process of composing music:

> When I feel well and in a good humor, or when I am taking a drive or walking after a good meal, or in the night when I cannot sleep, thoughts crowd into my mind as easily as you could wish. Whence and how do they come? I do not know and I have nothing to do with it. Those which please me, I keep in my head and hum them; at least others have told me that I do so. Once I have my theme, another melody comes, linking itself to the first one, in accordance with the needs of the composition: the counterpoint, the part of each instrument, and all these melodic fragments at last produce the entire work: *Then my soul is on fire with inspiration,* if however nothing occurs to distract my attention. (pp. 72-73, italics added)

Although Mozart did not acknowledge God as the source of his creative genius, he did use the words *soul* and *inspiration* to describe the process, and it is God who inspires the soul. Artists and composers whose works draw us closer to God may not recognize his hand in their creations because they look to others as their more immediate sources of inspiration.

Others as sources of inspiration. We can be inspired by another person's character, integrity, or capacity to love through his or her actions or words. Stories told and retold can inspire, particularly those of our ancestors. As we read about the trials they endured and the sacrifices they made for their children, we may be inspired to move forward ourselves, knowing that our present lot is far less burdensome than the one they had to bear.

I am inspired most by those who are closest to me. They know me, and I know them. We recognize each other's weaknesses but look beyond them to the potential that resides deep inside. And when that potential becomes transparent, when someone says or does something that reminds us of our oneness with God, we are inspired to reach for something higher than we are presently capable of attaining. These moments bring peace to the soul, teach us who we really are, and inspire us. A simple act of kindness can breathe life into the recipient of the deed as well as into a quiet observer. Simplicity itself can inspire.

Shortly after our youngest child was born, my wife became seriously ill and had to be hospitalized. We had five children under ten years of age at the time. My first concern, of course, was for my wife's well-being, but I also needed to care for the five children. At a low point one day when I wondered if things were going to work out, a good friend came to visit. He asked about my wife's condition, and then he put his hands on my shoulders and said, "Now I want to know how you're holding up." It was a simple act, but one that I needed at that particular moment, and I think he knew that I needed it. His kindness breathed a little life back into me. And even as I write about it, I re-experience the inspiration that a friend can bring.

I saw my friend as a child of God and began to understand how, as we recognize each other as the offspring of God, we also recognize all of God's creations as his gifts to us that he has entrusted to our care and stewardship. When we come close to God's creations, we can receive a unique kind of inspiration. The artist Georgia O'Keeffe felt compelled to capture the image she saw from her window when she took her first plane ride. She was so intrigued by the beauty of the clouds floating effortlessly below the plane that she rearranged her garage and constructed an eight-foot by twenty-four-foot canvas so that she could paint the image of clouds against a blue sky *(Sky Above Clouds IV)*. We have all felt the inspiration that can come from being close to nature. It is no coincidence that Joseph Smith, the Mormon prophet, chose a grove of trees when he went to ask God for greater wisdom. Joseph learned that all inspiration that draws us to truth ultimately comes from God, and that while God may work through others, he is ultimately the only source of truth and light.

CONDITIONS FOR INSPIRATION

Just as we must seek inspiration, we must be prepared to receive it when it comes.

On the pathway to truth. Inspiration comes most freely when we are on the pathway to truth, when a question of the heart is guiding our search. Paul's encounter with the Lord on the road to Damascus illustrates the point. The Biblical account gives no indication that Paul was searching for truth or that he was readying himself to hear God's voice. But his immediate acceptance of God's counsel suggests that he may already have begun wondering about his practice of persecuting the disciples, a practice that he planned to continue when he reached Damascus. But the light he received changed his intentions. His march to Damascus, although it did not begin as such, became Paul's pathway to truth, which led Paul to become one of the most powerful witnesses in the old world to Christ's divinity, so powerful that upon hearing Paul's testimony King Agrippa said, "Almost thou persuadest me to be a Christian" (Acts 26:28).

Although our pathway will not be like Paul's, we must each find our way to truth, allowing our question to fuel our search. The inspiration we receive along the way may not come in the same form as Paul's, but as long as it ties us to God, as Paul's vision did, it can have the same effect on us as Paul's vision had on him. We can know Christ as he knows us.

A ready heart. Paul's heart must have been ready to receive new light; otherwise he would have ignored the vision and gone on his way. As we seek truth with our whole soul, inspiration will come—not necessarily in the way or at the time we would prefer, but it will eventually come, and it will change us as it changed Paul's heart from one that was "kicking against the pricks" to one of a faithful disciple.

Recognition. Paul recognized immediately the source of his vision. He immediately accepted the Savior when Christ announced, "I am Jesus whom thou persecutest." We are sometimes much slower to recognize inspiration when it comes to us. And even though it may come less directly to us than it did to Paul, we are still under the same obligation to recognize its source. Only when we recognize inspiration as coming from God can we understand our relationship to the infinite and prepare ourselves to receive greater truth.

RESULTS OF INSPIRATION

When we have sought and received inspiration, we will then appreciate the fruits of inspiration.

Increased purpose and direction. Paul's vision completely changed his direction in life. It taught him who he really was and helped him understand for the first time his true mission. Few will experience the instant change of direction that Paul encountered, but all of us can experience the constant course corrections that can come through inspiration. Some of this inspiration may grow out of personal victories we encounter along our pathway to truth.

Personal victories need not be of grand proportion to inspire us. While my family and I were living in France, we found that we savored the small successes with the language and culture—finding the fastest way to travel by metro and train through the city, communicating with the local grocer, understanding the person on the other end of the telephone, finding the right school supplies in a maze of aisles and shelves. Each success, no matter how small, gave us added strength to tackle the next problem.

Adjusting to a foreign culture is similar in some ways to going through childhood all over again. Like the young child who is excited about the simplest of accomplishments, the adult adjusting to a foreign culture must learn to celebrate the small victories. And as the young child gradually comes to understand the higher purposes of life, so the youth and adult must continually search for their own purpose for being. Bateson (1994) writes of "knowing in a moment that this is where I belong, for this I was created."

(p. 200); or in theological terms, "this is what I was foreordained to accomplish." These are powerful moments and must not be minimized or ignored. They are the moments that give our life direction and meaning, the moments that propel us to do what was once considered impossible, but they are also moments of peace that can come when we know that we are listening to the Lord, that he acknowledges us as his children, and that our future is ultimately in his hands.

Increased capacity to contribute. When we know our mission in life, we are prepared to make a greater contribution. Some go through life never quite knowing what they should do with their time, where they should place their devotions. They turn cynical in their later years, coming to the conclusion that there is no purpose to existence—not for themselves and not for anyone else. They come to see everyone's motives as purely selfish and hence become selfish too. They die never having recognized the inspiration that was available if only they had opened their heart to it. They never sense the guidance that could have come to them through inspiration because they close themselves to its influence.

Theologians sometimes wonder whether inspiration might squelch personal creativity: if God puts the words in one's mouth, where is the room for individuality? (See Talmage, 1977, p. 509.) But anyone who has read sacred text knows that Isaiah speaks differently under God's inspiration than does Paul. Inspiration liberates rather than narrows our individual capacity to create, and as it frees our creative powers, it prepares us to make the unique contributions that we were intended to make.

The most meaningful inspiration that we receive comes as we are attempting to help another person: the inspiration a mother and father sense for their children, the inspiration teachers receive for their pupils. In *Lorenzo's Oil*, the father, after much study and struggle, has a troubling dream that eventually results in a cure for his son's disease. Some would say the father experienced intuition, others that he had a sudden insight; I prefer to say that he received inspiration. He was trying to do more than find a scientific explanation for fatty acid absorption; he was in all reality trying to bless his son, and so the inspiration came.

Conclusion

Teaching and learning both require inspiration. When a teacher draws a student closer to truth, the teacher breathes life into the student, and when the student acts on the truth, the student breathes life into the teacher (see Doctrine & Covenants 50:22). Both inspire and are inspired as they engage in the education of the heart. They recognize that the inspiration they receive from each other comes from God, the ultimate source of all truth and light. They know the truth that comes to them is as necessary to the life of their soul as God's breath was to Adam's soul—that they cannot be whole human beings without being one with God and with each other.

When either teachers or learners lose their direction— when they seek external rewards more than truth—inspiration is blocked and the education of the heart ceases. If materialism and self-centeredness take over, the breath of life cannot enter, and the soul withers. As the soul shrinks, people lose their sensibilities, their power to discern and to love, their reverence for life, their humility, and their ability to edify or be edified. The learning that could be inspiring becomes sterile and pointless.

But when as learners we seek answers to real questions, and as teachers we tie ourselves to truth, external rewards and constraints lose their controlling influence, inspiration comes, and the soul is enriched. This is the kind of education that happens far too seldom in day-to-day lives. It is the kind of education that could change the world because it is the kind of education that can change the heart (see Mosiah 5:1-2).

Watchwords

• Inspiration is a more important fruit of good education than is intuition or insight. Inspiration "tastes" better than these other fruits because it brings us nearer to our Creator, the ultimate source of all inspiration.

• When we are on our own pathways to truth, as Paul was on the road to Damascus, inspiration will come freely because we are following God's will for us; we have made our hearts ready.

• Inspiration can teach subtly or powerfully. It can lead to a new understanding, or it can cause us to completely change our direction in life. In either case, one must recognize that the learning is coming from God.

• Recognizing the source of inspiration helps one to guard against cynicism because it strengthens the "rope" attached to the anchor of testimony.

• As parents and teachers are attempting to help a child or student, they often experience their most important moments of inspiration. This is the way God helps his children to "feed his sheep."

CHAPTER TWELVE

JOY

And as I partook of the fruit thereof it filled my soul with exceedingly great joy; wherefore, I began to be desirous that my family should partake of it also; for I knew that it was desirable above all other fruit. (1 Nephi 8:12)

When students in my college courses introduce themselves at the beginning of each semester, I have often asked them to describe their most fulfilling and most frustrating learning experiences. "What are the learning experiences that have affected you most deeply," I ask them, "both in positive and in negative ways? Think back as far as you can remember, and include any experience you desire—whether it occurred in a school or in some other setting."

The variety and richness of students' responses have often astonished me. While describing her most negative experience, one young woman told the class how her third-grade teacher had unleashed a box of snakes in the classroom, allowing them to slither along the floor under the children's feet, causing the whole class to scream incessantly. Another student recalled how she had been locked inside a closet for an entire morning by her kindergarten teacher—an experience that she believed caused her to have continuing problems with claustrophobia. Still another described how his older brother had made fun of his athletic ability when they were growing up—to the point that he never learned to enjoy sports, even as an adult.

Students' positive experiences have been equally compelling. One student told the class that her most fulfilling learning had come in her home with her family—that she looked to parents and siblings as her greatest teachers. A young man described the sailing lessons that he had taken recently and explained how the experience had taught him as much about himself as it had about sailing. Another student discussed how he and other students had enjoyed his science course so much the previous semester that on the final day of class all of the students rose simultaneously to give the professor a standing ovation. Describing his impressions of this professor, the student said, "I'm not sure if I will remember everything I learned about science last semester, but I will remember the example that this professor set for all of us. He wasn't just a good teacher, he was a good person."

As students shared their positive and negative experiences, they often told their stories with a sense of conviction that seldom accompanies classroom communication. Many of the students' accounts had taken on meaning in their life, sometimes greater meaning than the students realized at the time of the experience. I became so intrigued with the nature of their responses that I invited a student to work with me on a questionnaire that we administered to 165 students, asking them—as I had the students in my own classes—to describe their most fulfilling and most frustrating learning experiences (Top & Osguthorpe, 1985). Results showed that most of the fulfilling experiences occurred outside formal educational settings, while most negative experiences occurred inside the walls of a school.

Looking back on this particular study I wonder why we used the word *fulfilling* to describe the student's most positive experience. "Why," I ask myself, "didn't we use the word *joy?*" I do not remember considering the word at the time, but if we did consider it, I believe we may have rejected it for the same reasons so many reject the other words that describe the fruits of the education of the heart. As we have discussed, words like *sensibility, reverence, humility, edification,* and *inspiration* have largely fallen out of usage in describing teaching and learning because they simply do not fit into the positivist tradition; they can not be easily quantified. As explained in chapter three, the word *love* has continued to be used but often inappropriately, in ways that can actually lead learners away from the truth they seek. But the word *joy* may be the most misunderstood of all.

Joy, for example, is often used to refer to sensual pleasure or gratification; consider, for example, books such as *The Joy of Sex* and *The Joy of Cooking*. But is joy the same as pleasure? Is there a difference between joy and happiness? We often say that we need to bring joy into the learning process—the kind of joy that young children experience when they make a new discovery. But do children experience joy—the same kind of joy that adults experience? Is the kind of learning that children experience the kind of learning we hope to experience in adulthood? I am convinced that the word is misused so often that most have forgotten the real meaning of the word *joy*.

From prophetic utterance we learn that if Adam and Eve had never partaken of the fruit, "they would have remained in a state of innocence, having no joy, for they knew no misery; doing no good, for they knew no sin" (2 Nephi 2:23-25). While in a state of innocence, Adam and Eve could not experience joy because they could not *learn*—at least about the things that mattered most, the things that would bring them joy. From the beginning of humanity, learning has been inseparably connected with joy. Simply gaining knowledge, however, does not bring joy. Joy comes from attaching ourselves to truth, cleaving to virtue, and allowing God to enter our heart and to change us.

The scriptural passage also teaches us that joy is not the opposite of unhappiness, it is the opposite of misery and grief. As Arthur Henry King (1986) has said:

> Now I came to understand that grief and joy are predicated upon one another—that we cannot know joy unless we know grief. That is why I am worried about those who are content with contentment. Content versus discontent is too slight an opposition, and does not produce psychic tension. It is a facile soul that can be content in the world as it is, and even if we do not have griefs in our personal lives (and most of us have, if we face them, although we may pretend they are not there), we have plenty of grief around us in the appalling condition of the world (p. 27).

When we think of grief, we often think of tragedies—perhaps an earthquake, a flood, or an automobile accident. But these are not the real tragedies of our day—there is only one real tragedy, and it is sin (see Kimball, 1945, p. 5). Natural disasters may claim the physical lives of thousands of victims, but sin claims the spiritual lives of those who become entrapped in its entangling grip. The daily newspaper is filled with examples of the grief that comes from sin—people unable to control their passions, who have sold themselves for temporary pleasures and gratification. These examples teach us that the only way to experience joy is to live righteously; to recognize sin for what it is; to admit that deceit, greed, and haughtiness always have been and ever will be wrong and will eventually lead to grief; and that sensibility, reverence, humility, edification, and inspiration (the fruits of the education of the heart) always have been and will forever be right—leading us to joy.

Just as there are multiple impostors for each of the fruits described in earlier chapters, contentment is not the only impostor of joy; comfort is another. We want our homes and our places of work to be comfortable. For example, the apartment building we lived in for four months while in Europe was described as an *endroit très agréable* ("a very pleasant place"), a place sheltered from the noise of the city, where we did not need to worry about pulling weeds because they were pulled by the grounds crew, and a place where one could live for years without being called upon to help one's neighbors—or even to learn their names. But I believe that the early Mormon pioneers or the Jews who resettled Jerusalem had more joy as they were crossing the plains or waiting in resettlement camps than many now have in modern apartment complexes. The pioneers and Jews knew what they were seeking: Zion. They believed that whatever hardships came to them would be worth enduring, and they had faith that God would sustain them in their trials and eventually would lead them to a place where they could live true to their beliefs. They were not seeking comfort, and they did not find comfort as we know it. But now that we are surrounded with every conceivable convenience, we may have forgotten what we are seeking (unless it is greater comfort); we may have little tolerance for trials when they come, and we may have lost faith in the Lord's sustaining influence. Many have arrived at a point where they know what *comfort* feels like, but they don't know what it means to experience *joy.*

Like Adam and Eve, the Mormons and the Jews were forced to leave comforts behind and face the harshness of an untamed world. They learned what it meant to experience grief and what it meant to experience joy. They were not innocent, as a small child is innocent. They knew firsthand the effects of evil, and they could sense its stark contrast with the good. When I see young children approach learning with eagerness—when I see their faces light up as they achieve something for the first time—I wonder why learning for adults cannot be similar, why adults can't explore the world with the same enthusiasm as a five-year-old. But childhood (at least as it was meant to be) is in one sense like the garden was for Adam and Eve—a place of safety where one is nurtured. In such a place one may experience comfort, even some measure of contentment, but one does not experience joy in its full sense.

Joy is transcendent; it is not hemmed in by the frailties of the flesh. It must be experienced by the whole heart, the whole soul— by one who in complete freedom has chosen virtue, who in a world of hate has learned love. Joy can come only after we have tasted the other fruits of the education of the heart—when our sense of discernment has been quickened, when we have gained a reverence for truth and for beauty, when we have learned humility, and when we have been edified and inspired. Joy is the ultimate, all-encompassing fruit of the education of the heart. It is not an invention of the psyche but a unifying motion of the soul that fills us to overflowing, and we know that we are enfolded in the arms of God.

When we experience joy, we often cannot contain ourselves; we cannot find words to express what we sense. Joy demands more than words. Because it is an experience of the whole soul, we may feel a need to find new ways to express it. David of the Old

Testament shouted for joy, sang, and danced. A blessing that came to Job caused "the widow's heart to sing for joy" (Job 29:13). And while some may want to exult, others may feel tears of joy coursing down their cheeks. These deepest experiences of joy are uniquely individual. Everyone experiences them in different ways. They are redemptive feelings as we know that we can be free from the evils that sometimes seem to engulf us (see Alma 5:26).

But this does not mean that we can feel joy only when we have come face-to-face with our ultimate destruction; neither does it mean that all experiences of joy are times of uncontrolled exultation. Joy can come quietly in tones that are subdued and peaceful. A single thought can bring with it a soul-filling moment of joy. But whether the joy is overpowering or subtle, whether it brings laughter or tears, it always ties us more securely to truth, brightening our hope and expanding our faith. This is why experiencing joy is so much greater than experiencing contentment or comfort—feelings that are limiting and temporary.

Experiences of joy remind us that we are eternal—that we had no beginning and that we will have no end—and that as eternal beings we are co-creators with God. Romain Rolland has said that "there is no joy but in creation" (Rolland, 1910, p. 364). When we are creating, we are following in the footsteps of the creator. It is everyone's purpose to create, to leave something to those who will follow. In the education of the heart all creative work is truth-seeking work, the kind of work that brings us joy. When a composer hears a new melody, an artist sees a new image, a poet finds a new phrase, or an athlete imagines a new play, all may be finding truth. Each one knows when truth has been found because the discovery, although it is new, seems familiar—like finding a favorite toy we lost as a child. For the musician the melody will endure if it is "singable," if it fits a pattern that is already inside the composer and the listener; the poet's phrase will find its way into everyday speech; the artist's image will be recalled by viewers even when the painting or sculpture is not present; and the athlete's play will become a part of the game.

The most sacred of all creations is the newborn infant, the joint offspring of God and mortals, the union of spirit and body into a new soul. It should not be surprising that many of the most grievous acts of humanity are acts that work against this most miraculous of all events—the birth of a child. As abortion, teenage pregnancy, and crimes against children continue to escalate, the family continues to disintegrate, and we face a complete unraveling of the society. But while our news media carry an unending array of stories about families that are failing, we must not forget that families are where we find our greatest joys. Families are the units that have the potential to endure—even though we see so many falling apart all around us. Families are the learning centers for the education of the heart where children can best be taught to ask questions, study, ponder, pray, and accept guidance. They are the places where we learn to experience more joy in another's success than we do in our own (Alma 29:14-16). Families are eternal schools of the heart. We will never outgrow our need to seek truth together as family members nor to help each other in the search. Like the prophet Nephi, when we find the truth that is "most desirable above all other fruits," we will want to share it first with our family (1 Nephi 7).

Even when families fail—even as families are "redefined"—the intangible ties of the heart keep the hope alive that family relationships will endure. I once asked a Danish family therapist to explain how her country cared for its abandoned children. She responded, "We have a strong feeling in Denmark that children who have been removed from their birth parents need to keep their relationship alive with these parents, even though they have been successfully placed in foster homes. We tell these children at times that their birth parents are unable to care for them because they are still alcoholic or drug-addicted, and are simply unable to care for their natural children." Pointing to her head, she then remarked, "These children understand the logic of our explanation in their head, but," she said, pointing to her heart, "they never seem to understand it in their heart. Their desire for contact with their natural parents never seems to die."

Families are uniquely designed to deal with matters of the heart; thus, the failure of a family is of grander proportion than the failure of any organization or institution designed by humans. Governments, on the other hand, are uniquely impotent in dealing with the matters of the heart—impeding moral development, for example, as often as they foster it. When I asked a Russian woman, who had been living in France for two years following the fall of the communist regime, if she would be returning to her homeland, she shrugged her shoulders as if to say, "I wish we could, but it's not likely." She went on to explain that the main reason she and her family were staying in France was for the benefit of her teenage son.

"We just cannot bring ourselves to take our son back into a country that is falling apart morally, a country where young people spend more time selling their wares on the street than they do studying. I don't want my son to grow up in that kind of atmosphere."

I responded by saying, "It will likely take a whole generation for things to improve."

"No," she said without hesitation, "It will take two generations, one to forget the old ways and another to learn the new."

In the education of the heart every question is a moral question, every search a moral search, and every act of guidance a moral act. There are no courses in moral development, neither are there courses entitled "The Education of the Heart." Diplomas cannot be issued for mastering a predetermined set of concepts; certificates of proficiency cannot be granted for passing a performance test. The education of the heart cannot be confined to fifty-minute class periods or to four-month college semesters. This form of education has no distinct point of departure and will have no finish line. When the Russian mother said that more than one generation would be required to reinstill moral fiber into her countrymen, I nodded and said, "It has to begin when the child is young." As she showed her agreement, I added, "From the moment a child is born."

She shook her head. "No," she said. "It begins even before that."

Because learning begins before birth and continues beyond death, joy is never complete. As long as there is any measure of grief in the world, we cannot have a fullness of joy, but as long as there is any measure of hope in the world, we can experience joys that know no earthly bounds. As my conversation with the Russian mother continued, she explained with conviction that all children need to "develop a sense of right and wrong inside themselves—and education is the only way to do this" and that "children need to read Dostoevsky; they need to learn to appreciate art. I don't believe anyone could ever kill another person if they had learned to appreciate art. But as long as the Russian government devotes only one-third of one percent of its budget to education, there is no hope." Then, as if she were wondering about her own assertion, she expressed her dismay over the Bosnian conflict. "How could something like this happen in Europe, where people should know better how to live with each other?"

I agree with the Russian mother that moral development happens inside each person and that education is the way to nurture such development. But not education as we know it. While government budgets may bring higher rates of literacy, they cannot teach discernment, reverence, or inspiration. Government policies do not edify because truth cannot be legislated; the role of government is to create and protect an environment where individuals, families, and institutions can foster faith, cleave to virtue, and seek truth. When governments attempt to do these things directly through legislation, the results will always fall short of the mark. The final answer lies not in passing new bills in the legislature on crime prevention, the family, or school reform. The answer will come only as we change the way we view teaching and learning by changing the way we view both the learner and the teacher.

Conclusion

We must come to view both learner and teacher in their completeness as whole human beings who must come to understand the connection between what they are learning and why they are learning it. This means we must dig deeper than we normally dig to find the relationships that underlie all searches for truth. Outward rewards must not be accepted as either the reasons students learn or the reasons teachers teach. The reasons for education are to prevent the recurrence of the brutality of the Holocaust—or any of the less visible inhumanities that destroy families and ruin individual lives. We are, as Gray (1990) has said, at a point in the history of the world that is "between hate and love." But the answer is not simply a course on peace education. The answer is not even, as the Russian mother suggested, art appreciation. We must have more.

We must recognize that we cannot experience lasting joy unless we place all our faith, nothing sparing, in the Savior. And if we have such faith and feel the power of the redemption as it washes over us, we can never rest, we can never assume that we will continue to feel joy with no time-outs. Everyone could ask continually along with Alma: "Can [I] feel so now?" (Alma 5:26)

When we continue to ask this question of ourselves we will continue to find truth. And finding truth we will act on what we find, and it will change us. Then we will know at least a measure of joy. And then we will understand why learning is a sacred privilege, an act of wonder—why when we are learning we feel most alive and closest to God. When this happens, we will have experienced the education of the heart.

Watchwords
• Joy is the all-encompassing fruit of the education of the heart. It comes as a result of tasting the other fruits. We feel a measure of joy each time we experience an increase in sensibility, reverence, humility, edification, or inspiration.

• Joy is not the opposite of discontentment or unhappiness; it is the opposite of grief. Only after we have experienced grief, can we know joy.

• Comfort and contentment are modern impostors for joy. One should never be satisfied with a life that is simply comfortable or brings only contentment.

• Joy is an experience of the whole soul—body and spirit. Sensing joy often makes us want to express ourselves in outward ways that are whole-souled. But joy can also come quietly and find expression in inward ways that are known only to the one experiencing it.

• Our greatest joys often come as members of families, the eternal units that allow us to be co-creators with God.

EPILOGUE

If ye have experienced a change of heart, and if ye have felt to sing the song of redeeming love, I would ask, can ye feel so now? (Alma 5:26)

Since I began writing this book, I have continually seen examples of the education of the heart in everyday life—examples that I had never noticed before beginning the project. I have been reminded of the time when I began working with people with hearing impairments and the surprise I felt to see how many in our society wear hearing aids. These people had obviously been wearing the devices all along; I had just never noticed them. It is almost as if somewhere deep inside we recognize that when we encounter a new idea, a new truth, we must make room for it—we must give it a place. And as it takes root inside us, we begin to understand in ways we had never understood before. We respond differently to those around us and to God because "all things have become new"; our heart has been changed.

I believe that such a change may occur not only when we turn away from error, but any time we embrace truth. Alma is not talking of a one-time event that happened in our past; he is teaching about the supreme importance of the present, as he counsels us to ask ourselves the question "Can [I] feel so *now?*"

The education of the heart has no beginning, and it will have no end. Everyone is automatically "admitted" to this kind of education; there are no limits or quotas. But the "open admissions policy" does not mean that everyone will experience the fruits of such an education at the same time or in the same way. Some will find their own questions more easily than others; some will understand the role of freedom and love in learning sooner than others; and some will engage in their search with greater faith than others. But the fruits are waiting for everyone who will enter the search and agree to persevere, even in the face of opposition or fatigue.

On a recent television news program, I was impressed with Thelma Sibley's moving account of the accidental death of her adopted five-year-old daughter, Nancy. Dressing Nancy on a cold morning, Ms. Sibley zipped up Nancy's coat and tied the drawstring on the hood to keep Nancy's head warm. Then when Nancy went down a spiral slippery slide, her drawstring got caught in one of the slide's joints and strangled her to death.

Following the accident, attorneys approached Sibley and told her that they could obtain sizable settlements as a result of Nancy's death. Rejecting their offers as immoral, Sibley chose instead to work with Ann Brown at the Consumer Product Safety Commission to pressure clothing manufacturers to eliminate drawstrings from children's coats and jackets. In essence, she became somewhat of an expert in consumer protection policy, learning, for example, that Britain had enacted a law against drawstrings twenty years earlier. To Sibley's surprise, her joint efforts with Ann Brown resulted in clothing manufacturers' voluntarily removing drawstrings from their products and including warning labels to parents about playground safety.

Sibley's story reminded me of the Odones' search for a cure to Lorenzo's ALD disease. In both cases, parents became committed to helping others avoid the suffering that they and their children had experienced.

LORENZO'S OIL, FERMAT'S THEOREM, AND LEVY'S COMETS

On my way home from a recent business trip, a woman from New York sitting next to me on the plane asked what I was writing on my laptop computer. When I explained that I was writing a book that would hopefully help readers remember the spiritual roots of teaching and learning, she described her own work as an editor of a magazine for practicing physicians and of a recent article she had written that focused on the role of religious faith in the practice of medicine.

When I mentioned my use of the story of Lorenzo Odone in the book, she said, "It's a great story to illustrate your point, but I guess you've heard that the medical community has some questions about the effectiveness of the treatment against ALD. But come to think of it, you're concerned about the way the Odones conducted their search more than you are about what they found, so the story is perfect for what you are trying to do."

I was impressed with her ability to comprehend so quickly the ideas behind this book. She was right: the search itself was what counted. And there is no doubt that even though the treatment that the Odones developed is not fully effective with all ALD sufferers, the work that the Odones began was an essential step in understanding the disease and developing a cure (see Moser, 1994).

While medical scientists have not yet found a final cure for ALD, the mathematics community apparently has come to agreement about the proof to Fermat's Theorem, a solution that has taken more than three centuries to find. However, the final corrections to Andrew Wiles' solution were not made by Wiles alone, but by Wiles together with his student Richard Taylor. As I read the account of Taylor's contribution, I thought how appropriate it was that Wiles' student became captured by the question and, in the end, helped his mentor come to the final solution.

For those who search the heavens, like David H. Levy, final solutions come in forms different from mathematical proofs. I recently watched on television a group of astronomers who burst into applause as a 746-pound probe from the spacecraft *Galileo* entered Jupiter's atmosphere and began transmitting messages back to earth about a place humans have never before explored. I secretly wondered if David Levy, the amateur astronomer, was among those who were cheering, especially when I heard that *Galileo* had taken the first, close-up pictures of asteroids.

In one of his recent books, Levy describes how his interest in astronomy was first sparked by his father, who gave him a book on the solar system and a telescope so that he could begin exploring the heavens. When as a young boy Levy actually saw the rings of Saturn, he called his parents out to look through the eyepiece with him. His father seemed as excited as Levy to see the rings. But by the time Levy had discovered his first comet in 1984, his father had contracted Alzheimer's disease and was too ill to understand the significance of the discovery. Although Levy deeply regretted not being able to share his most important "find" with his father, he continued to draw strength from their "first look at the sky together" (Levy, 1994, p. 242).

A BEGINNING, NOT AN END

When we give ourselves to the search in the way that Levy, Sibley, the Odones, or Wiles and Taylor have given themselves, our individual stories will write themselves, and as our education progresses, our stories will become richer and more rewarding, just as the stories in the previous chapters have continued to evolve. I am not a mathematician as Wiles and Taylor or an astronomer as Levy; my children have never suffered terminal illness or death as the children of the Odones or the Sibleys. Rather than searching for cures to rare diseases or comets in distant skies, I have sought to answer questions about the ways we should learn and the ways we should teach, questions I intend to keep pursuing the rest of my life.

Like the others I have cited, I am confident that my search will be enriched by those who lived before me, those who gave me birth, and those who are now accompanying me on my journey. From all of these I will draw strength. If I have moments when I feel that time or money is in short supply, I will remember my grandmother, widowed for the last sixty years of her life, who always found enough time to care for others and enough money to purchase a book for each of her grandchildren at Christmas. When I am trying to write and the words do not come, I will think of my mother, who, when she forgot the lyrics to a song she was performing, created her own rhyming lyrics without a pause—hoping that the audience was no more familiar with the original lyrics than was she.

When I am tempted to complain about the journey or to give up the search, I will contemplate the example of my dad, who for twenty-two years, never complained about the debilitating effects of Parkinson's disease, and I will remember my wife's father, who has never given up on anything. And if I forget the purpose of my journey, I will picture my wife's mother standing on the stairs in her family room, spontaneously reciting Moroni's words and imploring us to commit them to memory. As if performing a dramatic reading on stage, she would say, "And charity suffereth long, and is kind, and envieth not, and is not puffed up, seeketh not her own, is not easily provoked, thinketh no evil, and rejoiceth not in iniquity, but rejoiceth in the truth, beareth all things, believeth all things, hopeth all things, endureth all things. Wherefore, . . . if ye have not charity, ye are nothing, for charity never faileth" (Moroni 7:45-46).

Just a few weeks before I sent the manuscript for this book to press, my father died of heart disease in a Salt Lake hospital. As the nurse wheeled him into the room where he passed into the next world, he saw the window that overlooked the Salt Lake Valley and said, "Just open the window and let me go through." He was ready for the end to come.

Our other three parents are also approaching the end of their own journey, the end of their own search. But as Eliot reminds us:

> What we call the beginning is often the end
> And to make an end is to make a beginning.

That is why we must all engage continually in the education of the heart, even when we believe that it is time to let go. We must listen and learn and then wait and listen again, exercising faith and allowing charity to guide our every thought and act. Then our heart will hear the words of him who said, "I am . . . the beginning and the end" (3 Nephi 9:18). Then the answers will come, and what seems to be an end will actually be the beginning of another search.

> With the drawing of this Love and the voice of this Calling
> We shall not cease from exploration
> And the end of all our exploring
> Will be to arrive where we started
> And know the place for the first time.
> (T. S. Eliot, in Harmon, 1992, p. 993-994)

CLASS NOTES

1. The teacher who accepts the premise that students should follow their own questions of the heart teaches differently than one whose primary goal is to cover the curriculum. Parker Palmer has compared covering the curriculum to covering a baseball field with a tarp in a rainstorm: "Once the field is covered, it has been effectively obscured from view—no one can see the field any longer" (personal communication, 1992). In our attempts to cover the core curriculum prescribed for second grade or to cover every concept in a church lesson manual, we often obscure the most important truths to be learned.

When teachers avoid the trap of covering curriculum, they realize that they cannot legitimately invite students to ask their own questions unless they as teachers are allowing questions to drive their own learning as well. I recently participated in a project funded by the National Science Foundation in which secondary-age students joined with their classroom teachers and with scientists at the university to ask questions to which no one knew the answers. Rather than demonstrating scientific principles by performing experiments we had previously conducted, we did science the way scientists do it—asking questions that have not yet been answered satisfactorily in the literature. It was a new experience for students to discover that they were inquiring into something to which the teacher did not already have the "right" answer. Their role as students changed as they began to see themselves as fellow searchers with the teacher rather than as pupils who were trying to please the teacher by parroting back the correct answer.

Although our project focused on science education, I am convinced that the principle applies to all types of learning. Students need to see the artist, the linguist, or the basketball coach experiment with a new idea—solve a new problem that other artists, linguists, or coaches have not yet solved. If they regularly observe and participate in this kind of experimentation, students will develop their own questions more readily and will not be afraid to search for answers.

2. If we examine the current debate over freedom in education, I believe that we will gain insight into issues of freedom that face us in our role as teachers. Two authors who represent the extremes of the debate have helped me to see the contrast between those who call for more control and those who want to let students "go it on their own." Contrasting the experience of Sudbury Valley School with E. D. Hirsch's approach to cultural literacy helps to clarify the issues that underlie the education of the heart.

Sudbury Valley School

Greenberg (1991) describes how Sudbury Valley, a private school in Framingham, Massachusetts, has for nearly two decades given students ultimate choice and responsibility for their own learning. In this school, children determine their own curriculum. Teachers teach when students request them to teach. If a child is not interested in reading, no one in the school forces reading upon the child. Since learning about this school, I have asked myself how Randy would have learned to read at Sudbury Valley. My question is not unlike the questions parents of Sudbury Valley students often ask Greenberg when they visit the school for parent-teacher conferences. Greenberg might respond to my question as he has to the questions of parents:

> At Sudbury Valley, not one child has ever been forced, pushed, urged, cajoled, or bribed into learning how to read. . . . There has never been a case of dyslexia at Sudbury Valley. . . . None of our graduates are real or functional illiterates. Some eight-years-olds are, some ten-years-olds are, even an occasional twelve-year-old. But by the time they leave, they are indistinguishable. No one who meets our older students could ever guess the age at which they first learned to read or write. (pp. 31, 35)

At Sudbury Valley the teachers wait for the child to initiate the learning, whether it be in literacy, science, social studies, or any other topic. If the child does not request a particular topic, teachers do not teach it. Rather than being forced to participate in a teacher-directed lesson, students are free to choose *what* they will learn, *when* they will learn, and *how* they will learn. The issue of personal freedom is at the heart of the Sudbury Valley philosophy; the belief is that real learning can occur only when the student is free to make choices that are unfettered by state core curricula, standardized tests, or the coercive impact of grading.

Cultural Literacy

In stark contrast to the philosophy of teaching and learning espoused by those at Sudbury Valley is the belief that there is a finite set of facts that all must know if they are to be "culturally literate" (Hirsch, 1987). Hirsch makes a compelling case that the type of approach used at Sudbury Valley "enables [teachers] to regard the indiscriminate variety of school offerings as a positive virtue, on the grounds that such variety can accommodate the different interests and abilities of different students" (p. 21). Hirsch believes so strongly that this wishy-washy attitude toward curriculum is the central problem in today's schools that he has produced a *Dictionary of Cultural Literacy* (1989), and more recently books that define what every child should know grade by grade (Hirsch, 1991a; Hirsch, 1991b).

Hirsch's point is that the adult generation has an inherited responsibility to pass on the culture to the younger generation. He is not afraid of the issues of control or indoctrination because he is focusing on the enculturation function of education. He believes that the older generation is shirking its duty to the young, and that the only way to correct this is to define more precisely what culture we need to pass on and then to restructure our schools accordingly.

School is the traditional place for acculturating children into our national life. Family, church, and other institutions play an important role, but school is the only institution that is susceptible to public policy control. In the modern age, the role assigned to our schools is to prepare our children for the broader activities of society and to train them in the literate public culture. (Hirsch, 1987, p. 110)

Hirsch's position may appeal to those who have become frustrated with student performance that falls below that of other industrialized nations, but it has no appeal for those like the parents and teachers at Sudbury Valley who believe that our schools' most serious flaw is their emphasis on control and intimidation— their removal of students' personal freedom. In fact, what Hirsch decries most forcibly is what Sudbury Valley condones most adamantly: the child's right to choose. When Hirsch discusses reading programs, he cites P. S. Anderson's "self-selection" approach as the epitome of what is wrong with American education: "The self-selection program allows each child to seek whatever reading material stimulates him and work at his own rate with what he has chosen" (Hirsch, 1987, p. 113).

The evidence that Hirsch uses to show how our education system has failed could conceivably be adopted as a motto at Sudbury Valley because those at Sudbury Valley look first to freedom and second to specific content. Hirsch obviously holds to the opposite view; he looks first to the importance of content and then to freedom. The contrast is so blatant between Hirsch and Greenberg that Hirsch (1987) does not use the term freedom (except in a negative sense to show that it is the cause of our educational downfall) and Greenberg (1991) does not use the term curriculum (except in a negative sense—to show that it is the cause of our educational downfall).

As the original paradox would suggest, Hirsch, if he were to treat the topic of freedom directly, would likely say that it is the outcome of his approach—people can be free only when they know how to communicate, when they have learned what a culturally literate person must know. Greenberg, if he were to treat the topic of curriculum directly, would likely say that facts stuffed down one's throat have nothing to do with real learning; curriculum should create itself when the student and teacher alike are free to explore, wherever their desire for knowledge leads them. We might say that Greenberg focuses on the value of freedom, while Hirsch focuses on the value of truth. Both positions are compelling; both have merit; but can two such opposite positions both be right?

I have struggled with this question for some time. When Hirsch's book first appeared in 1987, I read it and liked it. I even bought his *Dictionary of Cultural Literacy* and used it to quiz my children and myself on his quite endless list of terms, phrases, and colloquialisms that "every American needs to know." And then, years later when a colleague introduced me to Greenberg's book, *Free at Last,* I again was intrigued with the powerful statement on the need to give students more freedom of choice in their learning—what might be called a freedom from indoctrination. But while both approaches are appealing, I have come to believe that both are incomplete. Hirsch gives us an incomplete view of truth, and Greenberg gives us an incomplete view of freedom.

When teachers experience the education of the heart themselves—when they are faithfully seeking truth—they will know when to "hold the hand" of their students firmly, when simply to show the way, and when to let go (see Child, 1995). Using this perspective, issues of freedom in the classroom become deeply human issues rather than issues of curriculum, classroom management, or behavior control.

3. A variety of approaches to learning has been tried in which students actively do something for someone else, something aimed at improving the world in which they live. Proponents of "service learning" or "project-based learning" believe that learning is particularly effective when students are trying to solve a real problem,

help another person, or contribute to their community (Kendall, 1990). Coles (1993b) calls this approach "doing and learning." It is the kind of learning my son Aaron experienced as he worked on the problem of alcohol advertising, and the kind of learning that students in our NSF project experienced as they tried to solve problems of air pollution, recycling, and wetlands development.

By the nature of their profession, teachers are engaged in "service learning" themselves. If teachers open themselves to the messages that constantly come from their own students, they learn how to serve individual needs more effectively; they learn how to solve real problems of teaching and learning. I believe that education advances significantly as teachers invite their students more often to experience this same kind of real-life problem solving by participating in service learning experiences throughout their formative years.

4. Reflection, as it is currently being used in the education literature, often focuses on the *self* rather than on the students in the teacher's classroom. Teachers are encouraged to think about the relationship between what students are trying to learn and their "past experience" or their "personal purposes" (Henderson, 1992, p. 30). Thus, teachers are trained to engage in positive "self-dialogue" and "personal confirmation." While this kind of reflection may help some teachers, it can aim them in the wrong direction. Like so much current educational theory, I believe that "reflective teaching" rests too heavily on the premise that the *self* is the ultimate definer of good pedagogy, and therefore the appropriate focus of a teacher's efforts to improve learning. I worry that the more we see the *self* as social scientists define it, the less we see the *soul* as God defines it. I am not saying that the reflective teaching movement has been a mistake—it has helped us to see important flaws in our ideas of teaching and learning—but it is simply not enough to lift us to the level where we faithfully seek for and respond to truth.

5. As teachers we want to see what our teaching has accomplished: What new skill has the student acquired? What new idea has formed in the student's mind? Which teaching method is more effective?

Questions about educational assessment abound. Parents want to know how well their child is doing in school. Administrators want to know where to "put their money—how to get the most punch for their education dollar." Politicians want to know how our educational system compares with Japan's, Germany's, or Great Britain's. "Will our children be able to compete in the global economy and the global community of the next century?" they ask (see Berliner & Biddle, 1995).

Educators respond to such questions by creating, administering, and interpreting tests. Whatever the topic, skill, or human characteristic, a test exists to measure its depth and breadth. We have developed such a fetish for educational testing that whole disciplines have grown up around the enterprise, such as psychometrics, educational tests and measures, and program evaluation. As educators we have come to depend on professionals in these disciplines much as those in the broader society have come to depend on tax accountants. We demand the services of a tax accountant or a psychometrician largely because of the artificially complex requirements of our tax codes and our state educational rules and regulations.

A professor of "educational science" at the University of Paris once described to me her dismay at the exaggerated importance of testing in the French educational system. She said:

> You realize that the *Bac* [the test all French students must pass before graduating from secondary school] is an institution in France. Who knows how much money we spend on administering this test to every one of our students who graduates from the Lycée? It takes three days for each student to complete the test—three full days—and that includes an entire day for the oral section of the exam with an examining team that has

been brought into the school from another region, all in the name of objectivity. But we will never give it up, never! The *Bac* is a permanent fixture in our system" (Danielle Zay, personal communication, September 13, 1994).

Creating tests to measure student learning is not a bad thing to do. Administering them to students is also not evil in and of itself. What concerns me is the way we use the results of the tests to classify, group, and label students as if they were products on a conveyor belt and we were the quality control experts, pushing some off the "belt" because they do not meet some preconceived standard. I may want to know how my nine-year-old child is doing in mathematics or reading, but I do not need stanines, percentiles, or any other kind of ranking number; I need only to know what my children know and can do, so I can help them progress.

The more sophisticated our tests have become, the less we seem to focus on the education of the heart. I am not saying that it is the fault of those in the educational testing establishment; they have just responded to the demands placed on them by the broader society. All of us collectively have called for clearer, cleaner measures of student performance, tests that will tell us exactly where a student or a teacher stands on a given topic or skill. But no matter how much time and money we continue to spend on educational tests, we are not considering the things that matter most, the things that cannot and should not be measured at all, the things of the heart. And the testing methodology itself can divert our attention from these more important things.

6. For the last century educators have looked at human beings as if they could be broken down into component parts, much like a modular entertainment system. Some have focused on the memory module, some on the recording module, some on the "input devices," and others on the "output devices." Science has always served as the model: first hard-core, behaviorist cause-and-effect

science, and more recently the somehow softer, cognitivist, "let's-admit-a-person-has-a-mind" science. But regardless of the philosophical position each "science" has been built upon, the human being remains atomized, incomplete, and misperceived.

As we have broken individuals down into their component parts, so have we broken knowledge down into its disciplines—which has led to a curriculum that is fragmented and incoherent. From kindergarten through college we learn mathematics in mathematics courses, language in language courses, art in art courses, and history in history courses. Because it has been that way in schools for so long, rigid divisions among the disciplines seem natural, even desirable to many.

Such a system has caused many students to believe, for example, that art is a discipline of beauty, mathematics a discipline of logic, biology a discipline of living organisms, and religion a discipline of morality. Most never grasp the beauty in mathematics nor the logic in art; most never see biology as a moral endeavor or religion as a commentary on living organisms because these aspects of the disciplines are not part of the course content. And even if an inspired teacher draws such connections, seldom are students encouraged to follow them all the way back to their origins, all the way back to truth.

Many believe that the way out of the dilemma is through *constructivism*, a theory based upon the belief that teachers do not pour meaning into students' heads; rather students come to understand a new idea by making their own meaning, bit by bit. Like intuition, constructivism is a reaction against behavioristic approaches that examine the learner's outward response patterns but refuse to examine the inner workings of the mind. Intuition and constructivism are both vast improvements over the beleaguered behaviorism that they are intended to replace. But while behaviorism ignores the mind, the current cognitive approaches ignore the heart. And because they ignore the heart, they cannot be considered holistic, even though their supporters may use the term.

REFERENCES

Allard, J. L. (1982). *Education for freedom: The philosophy of Jacques Maritain.* Notre-Dame, Indiana: University of Notre Dame Press.

Arnold, D. (Ed.) (1983). *The new Oxford companion to music.* Oxford: Oxford University Press.

Bateson, M. C. (1994). *Peripheral visions: Learning along the way.* New York: Harper-Collins Publishers.

Beering, S. C. (1990). The liberally educated professional: Preparing outstanding teachers. *Vital Speeches, 56(13),* 398-401.

Bennion, L. L. (1988). *The best of Lowell L. Bennion: Selected writings 1928-1988.* Salt Lake City: Deseret Book Company.

Berliner, D. C. and Biddle, B. J. (1995). *The manufactured crisis: Myths, fraud, and the attack on America's public schools.* Reading, Mass: Addison-Wesley.

Berthold, G. C. (1991). *Faith seeking understanding: Learning and the Catholic tradition.* Manchester, NH: Saint Anselm College Press.

Berry, D. L. (1985). *Mutuality: The vision of Martin Buber.* Albany: State University of New York Press.

Berry, W. (1989). *The hidden wound.* San Francisco: North Point Press.

Bloom, B. S. (1974). Time and learning, *American Psychologist,* 29 *(9),* 682-688.

Buber, M. (1965). *Between man and man.* New York: Collier Books, Macmillan Publishing Company.

Bloom, B. S. (1956). *Taxonomy of educational objectives: Handbook I. The cognitive domain.* New York: David McKay Co.

Bloom, A. D. (1987). *Closing of the American mind.* New York: Simon and Schuster.

The Book of Mormon: Another Testament of Jesus Christ. (1986). Salt Lake City: The Church of Jesus Christ of Latter-day Saints.

Boyer, E. L. (1993). In search of community. Washington, D.C.: American Association for Colleges of Teacher Education.

Butler, E. (1977). Everybody is ignorant, only on different subjects. *Brigham Young University Studies, 17(3),* 275-290.

Butler, E. (1986). A love affair with learning. Americana Collection, Brigham Young University, Provo, Utah.

Chilcoat, G. W. & Ligon, J. A. (1993). "Cheating is gonna get me through school": Circumventing high school social studies tasks. *Journal of the Scientific Study of Religion,* 16-17(2), 2-9.

Child, M. (1995). "Discipline": What shall we mean?: Reconsidering the personal, communal, temporal, and ethical meaning of "discipline" and "the disciplines" in education. Unpublished doctoral dissertation, Brigham Young University, Provo, UT.

Clark, J. R. (1946). Charge to President Howard S. McDonald, *Improvement Era, (49)* 1, 14.

Coles, R. (March, 1993a). The political life of children. Invited address at the Forty-Eighth Annual Conference of the Association for Supervision and Curriculum Development, Washington, D.C.

Coles, R. (1993b). *The call of service.* Boston: Houghton Mifflin Company.

Collins, A. & Stevens, A. L. (1983). A cognitive theory of inquiry teaching. In Reigeluth, C. M. (Ed.) *Instructional-design theories and models: An overview of their current status.* Hillsdale, NJ: Lawrence Erlbaum Associates, Publishers.

Cox, P. A. (1995). Seeing with new eyes. Devotional address, October, 10, 1995, Brigham Young University, Provo, Utah.

Dillon, J. T. (1988). *Questioning and teaching: A manual of practice.* New York: Teachers College Press.

The Doctrine and Covenants of the Church of Jesus Christ of Latter-day Saints. Salt Lake City: The Church of Jesus Christ of Latter-day Saints. 1981.

Dumars, D. (1993). Poet to poet. *The Writer,* October.

Eisner, E. W. (1993). Forms of understanding and the future of educational research. *Educational Researcher 22 (7),* 5-11.

Frankl, V. E. (1992). *Man's search for meaning: An introduction to logotherapy.* Boston: Beacon Press.

Gagné, R.M., Briggs, L. J., & Wager, W. W. (1988). *Principles of Instructional Design, Third Edition,* New York: Holt, Rinehart & Winston.

Gatto, J. T. (1991). Let's hear it from a guerrilla. *Across the Board,* 28*(7-8),* 37-42.

Gatto, J. T. (1992). *Dumbing us down: The hidden curriculum of compulsory schooling.* Philadelphia: New Society Publishers.

Gower, B. S. & Stokes, M. C. (1992). Socratic questions: New essays on the philosophy of Socrates and its significance. New York: Routledge.

Greenberg, D. (1991). *Free at last: The Sudbury Valley School.* Sudbury Framingham, MA: Sudbury Valley Press.

Gray, M. (1990). *Entre la haine et l'amour.* Paris: Laffont.

Gup, T. (1992). What makes this school work? *Time,* December 21, 62-65.

Harmon, W. (Ed.) (1992). *The top 500 poems.* New York: Columbia University Press.

Henderson, J. G. (1992). *Reflective teaching: Becoming an inquiring educator.* New York: Macmillan Publishing Company.

Hinckley, G. B. (1987). Lord, increase our faith. *Ensign* (for The Church of Jesus Christ of Latter-day Saints), November.

Hirsch, E. D. (1987). *Cultural literacy: What every American needs to know.* Boston: Houghton Mifflin Company.

Hirsch, E. D. (1989). *A first dictionary of cultural literacy: What our children need to know.* Boston: Houghton Mifflin.

Hirsch, E. D. (1991a). *What your first grader needs to know: Fundamentals of a good first-grade education.* New York: Doubleday.

Hirsch, E. D. (1991b). *What your second grader needs to know: Fundamentals of a good second-grade education.* New York: Doubleday.

Holland, J. H., Holyoak, K. J., Nisbett, R. E., & Thagard, P. R. (1986). *Induction: Processes of inference, learning, and discovery.* Cambridge: The MIT Press.

The Holy Bible: Authorized King James Version. Salt Lake City: The Church of Jesus Christ of Latter-day Saints.

Höss, R. (1991). *KL Auschwitz seen by the SS.* Warsaw: Interpress Publishers.

Imbs, P. (1973). *Trésor de la langue française: Dictionnaire de la langue du XiXe et du XXe siecle (1789-1960).* Paris: Centre Nationale de la Rescherche Scientifique.

Horwitz, S. & Castaneda, R. (1994). Student shot in Eastern High School. *Washington Post,* Thursday, March 10.

Joseph Smith's "New Translation" of the Bible. (1970). Trans. Joseph Smith, Jr. Independence, Missouri: Herald Publishing House.

Kendall, (1990). *Combining service and learning: A resource book for community and public service.* Raleigh, NC: National Society for Internships and Experiential Education.

Kilpatrick, W. (1993). *Why Johnny can't tell right from wrong: And what we can do about it.* New York: A Touchstone Book, Simon and Shuster.

Kimball, S. W. (1945). Thy Son liveth. *Improvement Era,* May issue.

King, A. H. (1986). *The abundance of the heart.* Salt Lake City: Bookcraft.

King, A. H. & Warner, C. T. (1990). Talent and the individual's tradition: History as art, and art as moral response. In J. M. Lundquist & S. D. Ricks (Eds.), *By study and also by faith: Volume 2.* Salt Lake City: Deseret Book Company.

Kolata, G. (1993). Andrew Wiles: A math whiz battles 350-year-old puzzle. *Math Horizons,* Winter, 8-11.

Kotlowitz, A. (1991). *There are no children here.* New York: Anchor Books, Doubleday.

Lévinas, E. (1993a). *L'étique comme philosophie premiere: Coloque de Cerixy-la Salle sous la direction de Jean Greisch et Jacques Rolland.* Paris: Les Editions du Cerf.

Lévinas, E. (1993b). *Dieu, la mort et le temps.* Paris: Bernard Grasset.

Levy, D. H. (1994). *The quest for comets: An explosive trail of beauty and danger.* New York: Plenum Press.

Lundwall, N.B. (1959). *Discourses on the Holy Ghost; also, Lectures on faith as delivered at the school of the prophets at Kirtland, Ohio.* Salt Lake City: Bookcraft, Inc.

Lynch, J. J. (1979). Living together, dying alone. Forum address, Brigham Young University, Provo, UT (October 23).

Maxwell, N. A. (1976). *Deposition of a disciple.* Salt Lake City: Deseret Book Company.

McDonald, K. A. (1995, March 24). A comet hunter's labor of love. *Chronicle of Higher Education,* A12-A17.

McEntee, P. (July 5, 1994). Wisdom of Samoan healers sought. *Deseret News,* B3.

Miller, G. & Enright, N. (1993). *Lorenzo's oil.* Los Angeles: Universal Studios.

Moser, H. W. (1994). ALD—Balancing hope against reality, *Exceptional Parent,* February, 53.

Nibley, H. (1989). *Approaching Zion.* Salt Lake City: Deseret Book Company.

Noddings, N. (1992). *The challenge to care in schools: An alternative approach to education.* New York: Teachers College Press.

Noddings, N. & Shore, P. J. (1984). *Awakening the inner eye: Intuition in education.* New York: Teachers College Press.

Nygren, A. (1953). *Agape and eros: Part 1: A study of the Christian idea of love, Part 2: The history of the Christian idea of love.* Philadelphia: The Westminster Press.

Oelkers, J. (1991). Freedom and learning: Some thoughts on liberal and progressive education. In B. Spieker and R. Straughan (Eds.), *Freedom and indoctrination in education: International perspectives.* London: Casell.

O'Donnell, S. (1994). Mind your business and pray, D.C. schools add police. *Washington Post,* Saturday, March 12.

Packer, B. K. (1980). The choice. *Ensign,* November, 20-22.

Palmer, P. J. (1992). Invited address, Brigham Young University, Provo, UT.

Palmer, P. J. (1993). *To know as we are known: Education as a spiritual journey.* San Francisco: Harper-Collins.

Pauwels, L. (1994). *Les orphelins.* Paris: Éditions de Fallois.

Postman, N. (1992). *Technopoly.* New York: Knopf.

Pound, E. (1951). *Confucius: The great digest and unwobbling pivot.* New York: James Laughlin.

Randel, D. M. (Ed.) (1986). *The new Harvard dictionary of music.* London: The Belknap Press of Harvard University Press.

Rasmussen, D. (1985). *The Lord's question.* Provo, UT: Keter Foundation.

Regis, E. (1987). *Who got Einstein's office?: Eccentricity and genius at the Institute for Advanced Study.* Reading, Mass: Addison-Wesley.

Robert, P. (1988). *Le grand Robert de la langue française.* Paris: Le Robert.

Rolland, R. (1910). *Jean-Christophe: Dawn, morning, youth, revolt.* New York: Henry Holt and Company.

Rorty, R. (1979). *Philosophy and the mirror of nature.* Princeton, NJ: Princeton University Press.

Rousseau, J-J. (1911). *Emile.* London: J. M. Dent and Sons.

Shulman, L. (1990). Aristotle had it right: On knowledge and pedagogy. Occasional paper. East Lansing, Michigan: The Holmes Group.

Simpson, J. A. & Weinere, E. S. C. (1989). *The Oxford English dictionary: Second edition.* Oxford: Clarendon Press.

Smith, J. (1985). The pearl of great price. Salt Lake City: The Church of Jesus Christ of Latter-day Saints.

Smith, J. F. (1978). *Gospel doctrine.* Salt Lake City: Deseret Book Company.

Smith, J. F. (Ed.) (1938). *Teachings of the Prophet Joseph Smith.* Salt Lake City: The Church of Jesus Christ of Latter-day Saints. 1938.

Suffert, G. (1994). Louis Pauwels: Le vertige du monde, *Le Figaro.*

Talmage, J. E. (1976). *Jesus the Christ.* Salt Lake City: Deseret Book Company.

Talmage, J. E. (1977). *Articles of Faith.* Salt Lake City: Deseret Book Company.

Teloh, H. (1986). *Socratic education in Plato's early dialogues.* Notre Dame, Indiana: University of Notre Dame Press.

Top, B. L. & Osguthorpe, R. T. (1985). College students' perceptions of their most fulfilling and most frustrating learning experiences. *College Student Journal, 19(3),* 222-226.

Travers, R. M. W. (1983). *How research has changed American schools.* Kalamazoo, MI: Mythos Press.

Webster, M. (1993). *Merriam Webster's collegiate dictionary: Tenth edition.* Springfield, MA: Merriam Webster, Incorporated.

Welch, J. W. (1988). Study, faith, and the Book of Mormon. *Brigham Young University Devotional and Fireside Speeches, 1987-1988.* Provo, UT: Brigham Young University Publications.

Whitehead, B. D. (1994). The failure of sex education. *Atlantic Monthly, 274(4),* 55-80.

Young, B. (1978). *Discourses of Brigham Young.* Compiled by John A. Widtsoe. Salt Lake City: Deseret Book Company.

Zwicky, J. (1992). *Lyric philosophy.* Toronto: University of Toronto Press.

INDEX

About the Author

Russell T. Osguthorpe obtained his Ph.D. in Instructional Psychology from Brigham Young University, and his distinguished career in teaching has led him to various universities, including the University of Paris, the University of Toronto in Ontario, Canada, and the National Technical Institute for the Deaf, in Rochester, New York. He has also served as an educational consultant for The China Disabled Persons Federation, Peoples Republic of China, the State University of New York at Stony Brook, the National Cristina Foundation in New York, the Office of Special Education and Rehabilitative Services, U.S. Department of Education, Washington, D.C., as well as school districts across the United States.

A widely published scholar, Dr. Osguthorpe is the recipient of the Outstanding Young Men of America Award and the National Cristina Foundation Founding Member Award as well as the World Is Our Campus Award and the Blue Key Professor of the Month award. He is listed in *International Leaders in Achievement*, *Who's Who of Emerging Leaders in America*, *Who's Who in American Education*, and *Who's Who in the West*.

Says Dr. Osguthorpe, "The idea for this book arose out of a desire to redefine learning and teaching in a way that would truly integrate the sacred with the secular, the mind with the heart. When we seek truth with our whole soul, we will deepen our relationship with each other and with the Lord, and we will experience learning and teaching in new ways." It is Dr. Osguthorpe's hope that this book will "help readers form their own questions of the heart, and study, pray, and seek guidance as they conduct their own search for truth."

Currently the stake Young Men president, Dr. Osguthorpe has also served in a variety of callings in the LDS Church, including branch president at the Missionary Training Center. While most of his callings have been with the young men in the Aaronic priesthood, he says that one of his favorite callings was when he and his wife were called to lead the music in Primary.

A native of Provo, Utah, Dr. Osguthorpe and his wife, Lolly, have five children. Familiar with American Sign Language, French, Taihitian, and Chinese (Mandarin), Dr. Osguthorpe enjoys foreign languages and choral singing.